Decorating with

Paint & Wall Coverings

Sponged walls serve as a soft background for furnishings. Information on sponging and other decorative painting techniques begins on page 48. Interior design: Orchard's Lazy K House. Decorative painting: Lauren Del Rosario.

Graphics painted over sprayed-on spatter paint liven morning workouts in this basement gym. Interior design: Sharon M. Campbell. Decorative painting: Susan Eslick.

Developmental Editor
Fran Feldman

Research & Text
Scott Atkinson
Christine Barnes
Christine Freeman
Susan Lang

Contributing Editor
Lynne Gilberg

Coordinating Editor
Linda J. Selden

Design
Joe di Chiarro

Illustrations
Bill Oetinger

Photo Stylist
JoAnn Masaoka Van Atta

Photographers: Dennis Anderson, 18; **California Redwood Association,** 111 top; **Glenn Christiansen,** 21 top; **Peter Christiansen,** 19; **Philip Harvey,** 1, 2, 4, 9, 11, 12, 14, 16, 20, 21 bottom, 22, 23, 24, 25, 26, 27, 28, 29, 30, 31 top, 36, 37, 48, 55 right, 62, 64, 65, 66, 67, 68, 69, 70, 71, 72, 74, 80, 94, 96, 97, 98, 99, 101, 108, 110, 111 bottom right, 112 left, 113, 114, 117; **States Industries, Inc.,** 112 right; **Western Wood Products Association,** 111 bottom left; **Tom Wyatt,** 31 bottom, 50, 51, 52, 53, 54, 55 top left and bottom left, 56, 57, 58, 59, 60.

Cover: Decorative painting on ceiling and French doors and a new color on woodwork coordinate with existing wallpaper to freshen up this elegant bedroom. Interior design: Kelly Heim. Decorative painting: Sara Harrah, Pat Fox, and Cecelia Yarnell. Cover design by Susan Bryant. Photography by Philip Harvey. Photo styling by JoAnn Masaoka Van Atta.

Walls That Work

Probably nothing can transform a room as quickly and completely as a new wall covering. By mere size alone, walls make a strong statement; whether that statement is muted and subtle or bold and boisterous depends on what's covering the walls. Knowing how to achieve the effect you want is a key element in a successful decorating scheme.

The best place to start is with an understanding of basic color and design principles, and that's where this book begins. Equipped with this information, you can then examine each technique to decide which material—paint, wallpaper, fabric, or paneling—will work best for you. Once you've chosen the perfect paint color, wallpaper pattern, fabric design, or paneling material, simply follow the step-by-step instructions for installing your wall covering—and enjoy the fresh, new look.

For her help in creating the section on decorative painting, special thanks go to N. E. Larkin of Fearless Faux.

In addition, we thank the American Cancer Society Designer Showcase, David Barnes, Jill Beardsley of The Beardsley Company, P. J. Bergin, Bradbury & Bradbury Art Wallpapers, Cal-Western Paints, Craig Steven Costa, Dake's Interiors, the Designer Showcase for the Benefit Guild of the East Bay, Sally Goggin, Patricia Gregoire, Joan Jenkins of Chaney's Paint & Wallpaper, the National Paint & Coatings Association, Pump House Painting School, the San Francisco Decorator Showcase, Bob Snyder, Craig Thurston, University Art Center, Mary Weiland of East Bay Paint Center, and Karen Winger.

Special thanks also go to Kathy Oetinger for cutting color screens for the illustrations and to Menlo Park Hardware Co. for supplying props for some of our photographs.

Editor: Elizabeth L. Hogan

Third printing December 1992

C O N T E N T S

A beautiful blend of color, pattern, and texture illustrates the elements and principles of good design. Ethereal glazed walls set the scene for an old-world look that combines neoclassical motifs and hushed hues; refined patterns maintain the serene mood. Interior design and decorative painting: Peggy Del Rosario.

Color & Design

DECORATING BASICS

Good design doesn't just happen, except in nature. Instead, design involves a conscious, subjective process of selecting and organizing materials and objects in a visually pleasing way. When well executed, good design is as functional and comfortable as it is beautiful.   But design is not just the province of interior designers and architects. Every time you choose a paint color, buy a rug, or arrange furniture in a space, you're making design decisions. Sometimes, those decisions come easily; other times, you may need help in choosing colors, materials, and styles.   That help is here. In this chapter, you'll learn all about color and how it works, as well as how to apply universal design principles to your own situation. With this knowledge, you can begin to develop your own sense of design through observation and practice. The key is to look—really look— at how color and design are used in the fabrics, furnishings, and even the buildings around you. Notice how colors are combined, how patterns interact, and how elements relate to one another in their placement.   The more you look, the easier it will be for you to narrow down your choices and determine what works for you. Then you'll be able to develop a successful decorating scheme that both expresses your taste and fits your life-style.

All About Color

Design starts with color. Whether you have strong preferences or not, color is undoubtedly your first consideration when planning a decorating scheme. Whatever your level of color confidence, take the time to read the principles that follow. With an understanding of the fundamentals, you'll know how to create a color scheme, set a mood, even alter the sense of space in a room—in short, how to make color work.

A couple of color caveats: Colors come and go in home decorating, just as they do in fashion, so avoid trendy colors that will soon look dated. Also, remember that color is enormously subjective and emotional. No two people see it the same way. Consider your color likes and dislikes and those of family members who will live with the scheme you're creating.

And finally, remember that guidelines are just guidelines, not hard-and-fast rules. If you want to experiment with unusual color combinations, go ahead, but work with the largest possible samples before you commit yourself to strong or offbeat colors.

A color vocabulary

To understand and use color theory, you need to know some basic terms.

Hue is just another word for color. Royal blue, fire engine red, and bright yellow are hues, as are such softer colors as dove gray, terra-cotta, and cream.

Each hue has a visual "temperature." Yellow, orange, and red are warm and lively; they're often referred to as advancing colors because they seem nearer than they actually are. Blue, green, and violet are cool and tranquil; they're called receding colors because they appear to be farther away.

The term *value* refers to the lightness or darkness of color. The more white in a color, the lighter the value; these colors, called *tints*, lie just inside the hue ring on the color wheel (see facing page). The more black in a color, the darker the color's value; these col-ors, termed *shades*, appear just outside the hue ring on the color wheel.

Color with gray added is a *tone*. Adding white, black, or gray to colors to make tints, shades, or tones is called *extending* colors.

Intensity is the degree of purity, or saturation, of color. Although both pale pink and bright red are technically red, they differ in their intensity, or strength, of color. You increase a color's intensity by adding more of the pure color; adding white, black, or the color's complement (see facing page) reduces intensity. Full-intensity colors are so strong and stimulating that they're usually used only for emphasis in decorating.

The color wheel

As you look at the color wheel, keep in mind that its colors are almost always altered and combined in ways that soften their impact.

All color combinations, from safe to audacious, come from variations and combinations on the basic color wheel. Although the color wheel can't dictate formula schemes, it can help you imagine what will happen when colors are put together. And, if you have a definite color in mind, the color wheel expands your choices by allowing you to build a number of different schemes.

■ *Primary colors*—red, blue, and yellow—are the source of all other colors. Primaries are powerful, usually too powerful to use at full strength on large expanses, such as walls.

■ *Secondary colors* lie midway between the primary colors on the color

Color Cues

You can develop an eye for color by paying close attention to color in nature, art, and design. Analyzing the relationships between colors in both natural and designed schemes will help you create your own innovative combinations.

Some of the most striking complementary color combinations occur in nature—red berries on holly, a yellow-orange sun behind blue-violet mountains at sunset. You can capture the beauty of your environment by borrowing hues from the earth, plants, and sky. That way your home becomes an integral part of your surroundings.

For unusual color ideas, turn to well-known works of art. As you study the colors in paintings by Monet, Gauguin, Matisse, and others, try to tease apart the color combinations, moving from the refined colors on the canvas to the full-intensity colors on the color wheel.

Finally, pick up color cues from your furnishings. You can build a color scheme based on colors in wallpaper, fabric, a rug, even a favorite needlework pillow. One reliable approach to choosing paint is to match the predominant color in a fabric or rug to a paint chip; then use the lightest color (or a darker one for more drama) on that card.

If you're starting from scratch, you can draw inspiration from a fabric containing colors you love. In a sense, the fabric's designer has already done the work for you by bringing together colors in a harmonious way.

A simple method of translating a fabric into a color scheme is to use the dominant color, toned down, on the walls, perhaps with a touch of it in the floor treatment. The next strong color can go on furniture or windows. Use the fabric's accent color in accessories. Just be sure to vary the quantities of color and to repeat each one at least once.

wheel because they're formed by combining primaries: green comes from blue and yellow, orange from yellow and red, and violet from red and blue. Secondary colors are less strong than primaries.

■ *Intermediate colors* result when you mix a primary color with an adjacent secondary color. Blue (a primary) and violet (a secondary) combine to make blue-violet, an intermediate.

■ *Tertiary and quaternary colors* add depth and sophistication to a color scheme. Look at the color circle at the lower right and follow the arrows to make the tertiaries: green and orange make wheat, orange and violet make brick, and violet and green make slate. Note that the tertiaries have had varying amounts of white added to them.

Combining tertiary colors creates quaternary colors: wheat and brick become sandstone, brick and slate become eggplant, and slate and wheat become juniper.

Subtle versions of the original colors, tertiaries and quaternaries are also richer colors than can be obtained by adding black to colors to make shades. For example, the quaternary color juniper, a combination of slate and wheat, is much more complex and interesting than green combined with black.

■ *Complementary colors* are those opposite each other on the color wheel. Red and green are complements, as are blue and orange, yellow and violet.

Complementary colors are stimulating and full of surprises. Used in their full intensity, they seem harsh. When mixed in equal amounts, they *neutralize* each other, forming a flat, neutral gray. But when a small amount of one color is added to its complement, the result is a pleasing, less intense version of the predominant color. The inner wedges on the color wheel show tints that have a bit of complement added, forming extended and neutralized colors.

With just small adjustments and the use of a range of tints and shades, intriguing colors can be formed. To orange, for example, add a small amount of its complement, blue, to neutralize the orange. To that color add enough white to make a tint best described as

■ LOOKING AT COLOR

Color wheel

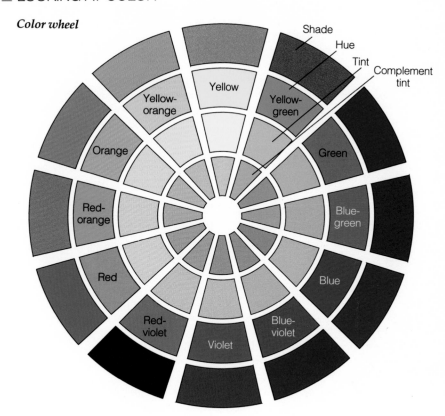

Color circle

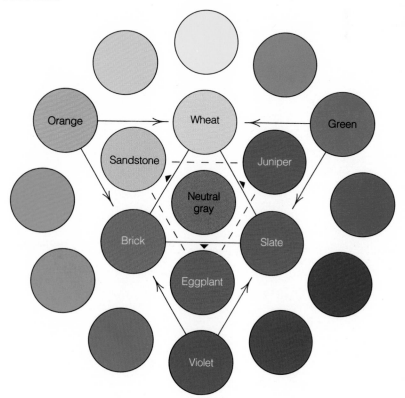

pale peach, appropriate as a quiet background color. Or mix in the opposite direction: to blue, add a bit of orange and a great deal of white to create a soft blue gray.

■ *Neutral colors*—white, black, and gray—are the noncolors. Although not technically neutrals, low-intensity warm colors such as beige and cream are usually included in neutral schemes. Neutrals make bright accents seem even brighter. Light-value neutrals are ideal backgrounds for furnishings and artwork, since they put the focus on what's in the room, not what color is on the walls.

Color combinations

Once you see how the different color combinations are formed, you can build your own combinations from a favorite color or colors. Even if the color combination you have in mind doesn't fit any of these schemes, it can still be a smashing success.

Remember: You don't have to think of colors in their full intensities. By neutralizing (adding a bit of a color's complement) and extending (adding white, black, or gray), you'll change the character of colors and form more sophisticated combinations.

Monochromatic. Monochromatic schemes—combinations that employ one color in a variety of intensities and values—are simple to put together and easy to live with because they're so restful. Since colors have so much in common in monochromatic schemes, rooms appear unified and harmonious. Contrasting values will create interest, but too much variation may look uneven.

A neutral combination, a type of monochromatic scheme, consists of white, black, and very low intensities of such colors as beige and taupe. Neutrals can be warm or cool, so try for consistency when planning a color scheme. To avoid monotony, use a range of light-to-dark values.

With both monochromatic and neutral color schemes, the use of accent colors and a mix of textures keep the effect lively.

Complementary. Based on any two colors opposite each other on the color wheel, complementary schemes are richer than monochromatic ones because they balance warm and cool colors (see drawing below, at left). These combinations can be startling or subdued. Look beyond such obviously jarring complements as intense yellow and violet to see the possibilities of quiet combinations, such as cream and amethyst (tints of yellow and violet, each slightly neutralized).

Varying the intensity, area, and value of the complements effectively avoids the clash of pure opposing colors. For example, you can balance a large area of pale, neutralized blue with a small shot of intense orange, its complement.

More involved complementary combinations produce more interesting color schemes. If these complex combinations seem shocking in theory, keep in mind that the most pleasing schemes result from neutralizing and extending the colors and using them in varied quantities. The structure of all complementary combinations ensures color harmony and prevents color chaos because the colors are automatically balanced.

A *triad* combination consists of any three colors equidistant from each other on the color wheel. Sound complicated? Think about the options and you'll see the potential for vigorous but balanced combinations. Equidistant colors orange, green, and violet may become a triad of refined colors we call cocoa, sage green, and dove gray; red, blue, and yellow may be interpreted as mahogany, French blue, and vanilla.

A *split complement* also contains three colors—one primary or intermediate color plus the color on each side of its opposite. Yellow plus red-violet and blue-violet is one example of a split complement.

A *double split complement* comes from splitting *both* sides of the color wheel. Instead of the split complement just described, also split the yellow to get yellow-orange and yellow-green. You now have four colors in a combination that's more dynamic and harmonious than either a complement or a split complement.

■ COMPLEMENTARY COLOR COMBINATIONS

Complement

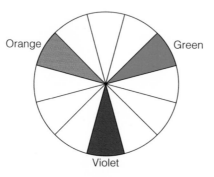

Triad

Split complement

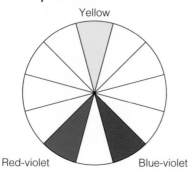

Double split complement

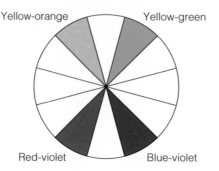

■ COLOR SCHEMES: FOUR EXAMPLES

A triad of quaternaries—sandstone, eggplant, and juniper—plus a tint of violet combine in a sophisticated jungle pattern.

Analogous combination of blue and green tints, shades, and tones is warmed by peach, blue's complement.

High-intensity hues from all around color wheel produce a bold, balanced scheme. Less-intense peach softens effect.

Impressionistic pattern is composed of primaries and secondaries that are similar in value and intensity.

Used in their full intensities, these are brilliant tropical colors. Refine them and the yellow-orange becomes a soft papaya, the blue-violet a pale lavender blue, the red-violet a quiet orchid, and the yellow-green a light lime.

Analogous. Varied yet harmonious, analogous, or related, color combinations are composed of two or more colors that lie next to each other on the color wheel. The most agreeable analogous combinations are limited to colors falling between two primaries and including one of those primaries—yellow-green, green, blue-green, and blue, for example.

This kind of color plan naturally develops when you begin with a favorite color and add related colors to it. But be careful not to combine too many colors (use four at most), and be sure to let one color predominate. To increase the interest in an analogous combination, extend the colors to form tints, shades, and tones. Then add small quantities of complements to provide some needed color punch.

Color characteristics

Colors have qualities that can work magic on walls. Understanding the characteristics of color will open up a world of design ideas and make it easier for you to choose the right paint or wall-covering color.

How light affects color. The quality of light, whether that light is natural or artificial, can greatly affect colors, which is why it's so important to examine a large sample of the color you think you want under different light conditions.

Cool fluorescent light amplifies cool colors and weakens warm ones; under cool light, a blue-base color seems more blue, but a yellow-base color appears duller. Warm incandescent light enhances warm colors while weakening cool ones.

Reflected light behaves in much the same way. Light bouncing off a cool green lawn into a room, for example, will have a different effect than light reflecting off a warm brick wall. Light tinted with a certain color will raise the intensity of similar colors and neutralize complementary colors.

Light also alters a color's value. Low light darkens value and reduces intensity; a higher light level lightens value and increases intensity. Too much light can make colors look washed out.

"Altering" space with color. A color's visual temperature can alter the sense of space in a room. Because such warm colors as apricot, yellow, and terra-cotta appear to advance, walls finished in those colors seem closer, making the room appear smaller. You can easily take advantage of this to make a large room feel more intimate.

Blue, green, and violet, on the other hand, are cool, serene colors that seem to recede; on walls, they tend to make a room appear more spacious.

Intensity and value also play a role in altering the perception of room size. More intense colors, whether warm or cool, make a room seem smaller; low-intensity colors visually increase the sense of space. Darker values (shades) of all colors diminish room size because they absorb light; a dark, cool color will come forward like a warm color. Unbroken expanses of very light values reflect the light and open up space.

Whatever the colors, intensities, or values, too much contrast has the same impact as a dark color—it reduces the perceived space. Conversely, harmonious monochromatic and analogous schemes enlarge space. Neutrals of similar value also seem to make the walls retreat, allowing the emphasis to fall on furnishings.

Ceiling color also affects the sense of space in a room. A ceiling painted the same color as the walls helps expand space. A darker ceiling, or a ceiling color that comes down the walls a bit, visually lowers the ceiling, producing a cozier atmosphere. A low ceiling painted a lighter color than the walls seems higher than it really is.

One of the simplest ways to impart a sense of spaciousness is to coordinate colors from one room to the next. But if your object is to divide space—for example, in an area that serves two different functions—use different colors and patterns in each area.

Color's effect on mood. As indicated by the color clichés—reds are stimulating, blues calming—color has the power to energize or to soothe. Although color "laws" are too general to be very useful, take into account the emotional impact of color when you're developing a scheme. Remember that walls, by their size alone, make a strong statement, whatever their color.

Sunshine colors (peach, yellow, and cream), light values, and high intensities raise spirits and brighten living spaces. These colors wear well in busy areas, such as kitchens and children's rooms, and mix easily with other colors. They're especially good in bedrooms and dining rooms.

Red, the hottest of the warm colors, has the power and drama of an afternoon or nighttime color. In rooms where the day begins—kitchens and bedrooms—red is usually considered too strong.

Note, also, that using a warm color in a south-facing room that's naturally light and warm may be overpowering; cooler colors and darker values will balance the mood and cut the glare. On the other hand, warm colors and light values will make a room with little natural light more inviting.

Colors midway between pronounced warm and cool (yellow-green and red-violet, for example), medium values, and medium intensities have a relaxed, comforting effect. These colors are appropriate in a variety of rooms. Cool, subdued colors (slate, forest, lavender), darker values, and low intensities are suited to formal, restful rooms.

Color as accent. Used as an accent, color effectively highlights and accentuates the architectural features of a room and the furnishings in it. Ceiling beams, moldings, wainscoting, and chair rails gain prominence when stained or painted to contrast with walls and ceilings. Light-colored furnishings will draw the eye when placed against dark, low-intensity walls.

Be judicious in the use of color as an accent, however. Too sharp a contrast can be jarring. If you want to inject clear, vivid color into a room, do so only in small quantities—for example, a primary-colored pillow or a bold quilt.

Just for Kids

Because kids grow so fast, it's a good idea to choose a wall covering that can grow with them, especially if you're not keen on changing the look often. Two other important considerations are practicality and durability. Spills, crayon marks, fingerprints, and other "accidents" are inevitable when children play. With all the choices available to you, you won't find it hard to select a wall covering that will stand up to a child's life-style.

One of the reasons decorating a child's room is so much fun is that you can use color so freely. Most popular for children are light and bright colors. Light colors tend to expand the room visually; they also provide a tranquil setting for the inevitable clutter.

If you want to decorate a baby's room in pastels, think beyond the traditional pinks and blues to other soft colors that don't say "baby," colors that will work for several years. Primary and secondary colors are naturals in school-age children's rooms.

Involve your children, if they're old enough, in your decisions. Ask them for their color preferences; then narrow down the possibilities and show them two or three color combinations. No matter how you approach it, keep the process low-stress and fun.

Paint. The fastest and least expensive way to transform a child's room is with paint. Solid colors show off favorite pictures better than patterned walls and won't compete with furnishings.

Sponging and dragging are simple decorative painting techniques that can add fanciful effects to plain wall color. Imagine a sky blue wall with sponged clouds or a wall dragged to create bold stripes. Stenciling a band of motifs at chair-rail height, where a youngster can enjoy the design, adds color and pattern without a lot of effort.

Murals and trompe l'oeil are the ultimate in paint effects for kids. Let favorite characters or special places, real or imaginary, take over a wall. Just don't make the design too intricate—large blocks of color are the easiest to execute.

Wallpaper. Wallpaper brings both pattern and color into children's rooms. For greatest durability, choose a scrubbable fabric-backed vinyl. A wallpaper border, with a companion paper or a solid-color painted wall, can add a decorative accent just where you want it—circling the ceiling, ringing the wall at a child's eye level, or outlining windows.

And don't neglect the ceiling. Whimsical designs, such as a starry sky or an expanse of clouds with birds, can lull even the most reluctant child to sleep.

Fabric. Fabric gives you a myriad of color and pattern choices. Stapling or pasting fabric on walls is a relatively quick way of covering them; when it's time for a change, the fabric can be removed easily. Choose a stain-repellent fabric, or apply stain repellent to the fabric after it's on the wall.

The Design Process

An understanding of basic design elements and principles will help you start the design process. Although the concepts may seem abstract, they need to be considered and applied as you develop your own style.

Elements of design

Color may be first and foremost among the design elements, but space, line, texture, and pattern are also critical to a decorating scheme. As you consider the many choices for walls, keep those elements in mind; they'll help you achieve a balanced, beautiful room.

Space. Walls enclose and define the space called a room. How space is perceived depends on how color, line, texture, and pattern are used.

Here are some ways to increase the sense of space in a room.

■ Emphasize openings, such as pass-throughs, doors, and windows, that let the eye travel through space to other rooms or to the outdoors.

■ When you're using textures and patterns on walls, keep their scale small to medium-size to make the walls look like they're receding.

■ Use light, cool colors on walls and ceilings, unifying the space with colors of similar value and intensity. Leave some expanses of wall empty.

■ Try trompe l'oeil effects on walls to create the illusion of depth.

Below are some ideas you can try when you want to make a large room or area feel smaller and more intimate.

■ Subdivide a large, undefined space into distinct areas by using a contrasting color, texture, and pattern on walls and furnishings in each area.

■ Use dark, warm colors on walls and ceilings.

■ Introduce rough textures on walls to advance them visually.

Line. The "lines" of a room refer to the room's shape or the dominant visual direction created by all the decorating elements. A room can incorporate many different lines—vertical, horizontal, diagonal, angular, and curved.

What you do to walls, more than any other aspect of decorating, establishes a room's lines. For example, the vertical lines in striped wallpaper lend a sense of height and formality to a room. Horizontal lines, as with horizontal paneling, add informality.

The isolated horizontal lines of a chair rail can break up expanses of wall for a cozier atmosphere. Diagonal and angular lines suggest strong movement, while curves impart a gentler sense of motion and energy.

Texture. The grain of paneling, the glow of paint, and the softness of fabric are a few examples of texture on walls. Even wallpaper, whether textured or not, possesses a visual texture.

Texture on walls is a subtle refiner of color. The smooth, shiny surface of high-gloss paint reflects light brilliantly, making color appear lighter and more lustrous. A surface with a flat, or mat, finish appears less bright because the finish absorbs rather than reflects the light. Decorative painting techniques, such as sponging and ragging, produce abstract texture that gives color depth.

The amount of texture you use in a room depends in large part on what you've done with color and pattern. A neutral palette or a scheme that includes very little pattern may allow for more texture than a complex palette or a scheme with combined patterns.

The key to working with different textures throughout a room is to introduce enough variety to create interest and modulate color, but not so much that visual chaos results. Try to strike a balance somewhere between bland and confusing. If everything in a room is sleek and shiny, for example, offset the

A quiet scheme gains texture from decorative wall painting, creative sewing, and varied accessories. Interior design: Mark Chastain and Susan Lind Chastain of Fine Custom Sewing. Decorative painting: Spike Lind (ribbons), Barry Nelson and Bill Sandoval (background).

smooth, reflective surfaces with a few soft, natural textures.

When you use texture, the scale should correspond to the scale of the room and its furnishings. Since texture tends to fill space, it's best to use small-scale textures—sparingly—in a small room. Large-scale textures work in a larger room and can even help reduce the apparent size of the room.

Pattern. Pattern brings rhythm and vitality to a room, unifying colors and textures with design. But the prospect of pattern on walls can be daunting, considering the possibilities in wall-covering materials. There are no pattern rules, but thinking about how patterns appear on walls and how they interact will make the job of choosing and combining patterns easier.

■ ***Pattern styles.*** Patterns vary in style and size. *Naturalistic* patterns are realistic renderings of natural forms, such as flowers; they're usually used in formal, traditional settings. *Stylized* patterns simplify and repeat natural designs to capture their essence; the

fleur-de-lis, a stylized iris, is one example. Stylized patterns occur in both formal and informal schemes.

Abstract patterns are loose, artistic interpretations of realistic designs; large, splashy florals are typical abstract patterns. Abstracts tend to set a contemporary mood in a room. *Geometrics* are nonrepresentational designs made up of stripes, plaids, and geometric shapes. Like abstracts, they're popular in contemporary settings.

■ ***Pattern scale.*** The size of a design motif when seen in relation to other motifs is referred to as scale. Small-scale or allover patterns have the softest effect. They're often used in small rooms where they're clearly seen and the design is retained. Used in larger rooms, some small-scale patterns are so small that they read like a textured surface, an effect you may want if you're looking for a soft appearance.

To keep a room from appearing too small, choose a pattern with an open, airy background; your eye will look through the pattern and beyond, making the room seem more spacious.

Large-scale, multicolored patterns impart a sense of formality and grandeur. A generously proportioned room will support large, brightly colored motifs, even when they appear on dark backgrounds. Because they have the effect of drawing the walls closer, large patterns can consume space and create the impression that the room is smaller than it actually is.

■ ***Line and pattern.*** The lines of a room will suggest how to choose and apply pattern. In a room with a high ceiling, avoid strong vertical patterns; instead, try a random pattern or one with a spreading design. Subtle vertical stripes can visually raise the ceiling in a low-ceilinged room.

In an angular room, patterns with dominant motifs will be broken as they go in and out of corners. A better choice to unify walls is an allover design with no noticeable repeats.

■ ***Combining patterns.*** You can mix a number of very different patterns successfully, provided they have a common color. Geometric and naturalistic patterns—stripes and florals, for example—are frequently combined. The trick is to unite all of the patterns with color yet keep distinct contrasts in their designs.

The same unity can be achieved by combining similar types of patterns in different scales, such as small checks and larger plaids. Again, a common color or analogous colors will help tie the look together.

Don't try to combine too many patterns in one area. A good rule of thumb is to use only one bold pattern in a room and use it on a large surface so that it predominates. Then add two or possibly three smaller-scale patterns, distributing them around the room to avoid pattern clusters that appear heavy or confusing.

Principles of design

Although these basic principles deal with intangibles, they're very important when it comes to decorating.

Balance. When a sense of visual equilibrium is achieved in a room, the design is balanced. To achieve balance, you need to think about the impact, or

Patterns mix beautifully when they have colors in common. Geometric floor covering and stylized chaise fabric share their colors with a naturalistic floral wallpaper. A pink table skirt completes corner. Interior design: Mona Branagh of Pacific Bay Interiors.

visual weight, of the elements in the room. Rough textures and bold patterns, for example, increase visual weight and attract attention. Small-scale furnishings and light, cool colors lend little visual weight.

Balance in a room may be symmetrical (where half of something is the mirror image of the other half) or asymmetrical (where visual weights are equal but not identical). Symmetrical balance is quiet, restful, and formal. Few rooms are completely symmetrical, but there are often symmetrical elements, such as a centered fireplace or identical chairs facing each other.

Asymmetrical balance is active, informal, and much more common in room design. In asymmetrical design, visually heavy elements are counterbalanced by less forceful ones placed farther from the center of the room. The same principle is at work in a pattern that balances visually heavy motifs with a grouping of lighter ones.

Rhythm. The organized repetition of elements in a design scheme constitutes rhythm. This repetition brings a sense of unity and continuity as your eye moves easily from one motif or area to another. While the repeated elements must share a common trait, such as color, for a sense of unity, they should also be varied to create visual interest.

A geometric wallpaper with a strong repeat design is an example of rhythm. More subtle rhythm comes from repeating the same or similar lines elsewhere in the room.

Emphasis. Emphasis suggests making some elements in a design more significant than others. If a work of art is the focal point in a room, for example, the furnishings and wall coverings should be subordinate. Without emphasis, a room looks monotonous; too many emphasized elements, however, will vie for your attention.

Scale. When the scale of a wall covering, for example, is in proportion to the overall size of the room, the room appears harmonious. If the scale is too large for the room, the effect will be overpowering; if it's too small, the design will look weak. You may want to

change the perceived size of a room by manipulating scale with pattern, as explained on the facing page.

Harmony. When both unity and variety exist in a room, harmony results. A careful combining of colors, textures, and patterns produces a unified whole. Too much unity, however, can make a room look boring.

Variety—in just the right amount—contributes vitality and excitement to a room's design. It may be subtle, as in slight variations in color, or it may be startling, as with sharply contrasting patterns.

One way to establish harmony is to unify walls and furnishings with a common color while varying the surface design from plain to patterned.

Decorating styles

Most home furnishings fall into two broad categories: traditional and contemporary. Traditional furnishings are linked inextricably with the past. Contemporary styles, on the other hand, represent original statements unconnected to history.

Note, however, that many of the pieces you're likely to find today blend traditional and contemporary elements for a look sometimes called transitional. For example, a heavily carved antique armoire may be reproduced in a transitional version that keeps the basic form but simplifies the lines. Or, a stern, 18th-century shield-back chair may be covered in a muted contemporary plaid that lightens the look.

Besides denoting the period of furnishings, the terms traditional and contemporary also refer to decorating styles. Rarely, however, is any room decorated totally in one style or the other. Instead, many people prefer what is commonly referred to as an eclectic style, one that judiciously mixes both the traditional and the contemporary.

As you develop your own look, be aware that the distinctions between traditional and contemporary can be blurred. Thus, it's perfectly acceptable to bring simplicity and lightness to classic styles, just as you can warm up a cool, contemporary look by adding soft, decorative touches.

Traditional. This is the style that's always *in* style. Traditional decorating transcends fads and trends and remains popular because it features the best from the past.

Actually a catchall decorating term covering many period styles from different regions and countries, traditional styles do share some characteristics: graceful shapes, a formal look, and a quiet order. The furnishings may be antiques or reproductions, but a sense of continuity with the past is always present.

Rarely, however, are traditional schemes exact re-creations of period styles. Instead, most people combine a number of traditional looks, choosing favorite motifs, colors, and patterns from different eras.

■ *Period styles.* Among the English periods, 18th-century *Georgian* produced furniture styles that live on today—Chippendale, Hepplewhite, Adam, and Sheraton. In French design, elaborate scrollwork and decoration characterized *Louis XV* pieces; neoclassical *Louis XVI* furniture featured straight lines and geometric motifs.

Although the American colonists copied English and French styles, a unique American design tradition emerged. *Early American* was a simple, unpretentious style based on European design but reinterpreted to reflect a more humble life-style. Typical designs were stripes and plant motifs.

The graceful *Georgian* period in America featured rich hues and scenic wallpapers. It's best exemplified in the architecture and furnishings of Colonial Williamsburg.

A third American period, *Federal*, was inspired by the neoclassical revival in Europe. Walls were painted plaster or covered with formal scenic wallpapers from Europe and Asia. Symbols of the eagle and classical motifs were prevalent. The best-known example of the Federal period is Thomas Jefferson's home, Monticello.

■ *Romantic.* The *romantic* look springs from a renewed interest in the Victorian era. Now regarded as excessive and flamboyant, the Victorian age made one important design contribution: the production of chintz. Garden

In this contemporary country kitchen, different but related patterns, a range of textures, and varied scales mingle successfully. Bringing ceiling color down the walls a bit visually lowers ceiling, adding warmth. Interior design: Thomas Bartlett Interiors of Napa.

and field supplied the motifs—fruits, flowers, and leaves—in colorful, curved forms. Many of those designs appear today in lighter, brighter colors and patterns. Pretty floral wallpaper and fabric capture the whimsy of this style.

■ *Country.* The continuing popularity of the *country* style illustrates the perennial appeal of a simple way of life. Originally, country was characterized by hand-hewn furniture, stenciled walls, and antique quilts, all of which reflected a return to the basics.

Today's *contemporary country,* the latest version of *American country* decorating, is lighter and less representational than earlier styles. Fewer accessories, larger and more impressionistic patterns, and light wood finishes bring the look up-to-date.

Two 19th-century furniture styles that ran counter to Victorian excesses now infuse contemporary country with clean, spare design. The first is the Shaker style, marked by remarkable grace and purity. The plain, pared-down Shaker pieces possess a timeless

quality and hint at the functionality and simplicity of 20th-century design. The second, derived from the Craftsman Movement, is the Mission, or Golden Oak, style. Larger and heavier than Shaker, the sturdy furniture of Gustav Stickley emphasized pure joinery and rectilinear design.

Several international country styles enjoy the same popularity as American country. The cottage garden and country house inspire the *English country* look, where floral chintzes cover overstuffed sofas and chairs in cluttered rooms. It's a relaxed, sophisticated style, loved as much for its comfort as for its beauty. *French country,* one of the most decorative styles, features exuberant hues and patterns. Also humble in origin, it has a charming simplicity reflected in uncontrived pine furniture and colorful Provençal cottons.

■ *Regional styles.* Such regional styles as *Southwestern* and *Mediterranean* make use of colors and forms that harmonize with the environment. Walls are more often plain than patterned; palettes range from muted to vibrant

hues drawn from land, sea, and sky. Art and accessories from the most formal regional style, *Oriental,* lend a romantic exoticism to traditional or contemporary settings.

Contemporary. From the curvilinear forms of Art Nouveau, the geometric patterns of Art Deco, and the functionality of the Bauhaus Movement came contemporary, or modern, interior design. In contrast to traditional designers who copied earlier periods, contemporary designers broke with the past to create a truly original style.

Today, the term identifies a style that's simple and strong. It's a spare look, one often described as high-tech and minimal. Furniture is regarded more as form than decoration; brass, glass, chrome, and steel are common materials. Open plans, the absence of clutter, plenty of light, and an underfurnished look all contribute to a sense of spaciousness. The palette may be neutral, pale, or bold, but the color is usually plain. When patterns appear, they tend to be abstract or geometric.

Because it's simple and spare, contemporary is the perfect style to highlight artwork or a beautiful piece of furniture. Mixing in a little old with the new softens the hard-edged effect.

Eclectic. Just as you can blend traditional and contemporary elements for a transitional look, so, too, can you mix distinctly different periods and regions for an eclectic style. But for the result to look integrated and sophisticated, you must aim for some continuity, some sense of purpose or order.

One way to accomplish this is to decide on the atmosphere you want—formal or informal—and maintain that mood as you decorate. Another way to combine a variety of pieces is to repeat a particular color or pattern throughout the room. A unifying color can pull together an assortment of furnishings and accessories; repeating a pattern will de-emphasize disparate shapes and achieve a coordinated look.

One of the benefits of a room decorated in an eclectic style is that everyone feels at home there. And it's the easiest style to add to as you find new pieces or inherit old ones.

Focus on Walls

An examination of your own home, as well as inspiration drawn from other sources, will help you decide on a wall treatment that's right for you.

Getting started

Begin by taking stock of your home and its furnishings, noting what you like and don't like about them. Then turn to such sources as home design magazines and books, decorators' showhouses, home improvement centers, paint and wallpaper stores, and fabric stores. And don't overlook your friends' homes for inspiration—the best ideas may be close at hand.

Once you're aware of your preferences and the choices available to you, turn your attention to the "givens." What is the style of your home? The best interior design takes its direction, even in a general sense, from the exterior design. Then look at your existing furnishings. Whether you're keeping what you have or changing things, the walls need to complement your furnishings.

How much light enters your home? If a room receives minimal natural light, keep the wall color light. Also consider the room's use; often, this will dictate the appropriate wall-covering material.

What is the condition of your walls? Some wall coverings demand completely smooth surfaces; others can go over less than perfect walls. (The how-to section for each wall covering will tell you what's required.)

Choosing a technique

Each wall covering—paint, wallpaper, fabric, and paneling—has practical as well as aesthetic qualities. Here's a brief overview. For more help, glance through each chapter to get a sense of what's involved and what can be achieved.

Paint. By far the easiest, least expensive, and most popular way to transform a room is with paint. Basic painting, done with a brush and roller, pro-duces a uniform overall finish. With the right paint correctly applied, even a novice can achieve great results.

Increasingly popular today, fanciful decorative painting finishes lend new vitality and depth to painted walls. Techniques range from the very simple, such as ragging and sponging, to the more technically difficult marbling and wood graining.

Experimenting with paint color and techniques is easy. Practice on a small area if you're not sure of your skill level, especially when trying one of the decorative techniques. That way, you'll know if you can handle the job, and if you like the effect.

Wallpaper. When it comes to pattern on walls, there's nothing quite like wall-paper. The extraordinary variety in materials, styles, colors, patterns, and textures opens up a world of decorating possibilities.

Wallpaper does far more than simply adorn walls. It envelops a room in color and design, adding excitement to any decorating scheme. Wallpaper can help "furnish" rooms, such as kitchens and bathrooms, where there's little space for furniture. In dining rooms and living rooms, suitable wallpaper can set the decorating style and pro-vide a unifying background. In any room, ceiling or chair-rail borders can complement wallpaper or stand alone against plain walls.

In practical terms, wallpaper can last for years. You'll find wallpapers that are prepasted, washable, and strippable, features that make hang-ing, cleaning, and removal easier tasks.

Fabric. Applying fabric to walls brings texture, warmth, and beauty to a room. Upholstered walls, where fabric is ap-plied over batting, are especially soft and luxurious. Stapling or pasting fab-ric on walls is a simple and fast method of covering walls with fabric.

In addition to their visual appeal, fabric-covered walls have functional characteristics. Stapled and upholstered walls conceal minor wall imperfections; often, you can use fabric where you can't use wallpaper. Upholstered walls also provide some insulation and soundproofing qualities.

Note, however, that fabric-covered walls must be well executed to look good. Neat, careful work counts. And even though most fabric suitable for walls is stain repellent, fabrics can't be scrubbed as many wallpapers and paints can.

Paneling. Wood works in many set-tings, from a formal dining room to a distinctive library or cozy family room.

The two main types of paneling, sheet and solid board, come in a vari-ety of textures and finishes. Whatever type you choose, the inherent texture and pattern of wood grain will bring warmth and character to the room. In addition, the strong design lines of ver-tical, horizontal, or diagonal board pan-eling can set a style and appear to alter a room's proportions.

Moldings can be used with or without paneling. They provide a vi-sual transition from one surface to an-other and create architectural details that break up flat expanses of walls.

Paneling is durable, easy to main-tain, and long-lasting. With it you can conceal problem walls that might be difficult or expensive to repair.

Need help?

For most decorating projects, an interior designer or decorator can provide the design expertise you need. These pro-fessionals work in a number of different ways. Paying the person an hourly rate may be the simplest arrangement, and the advice offered may be all you need. Other designers charge a percentage of the cost of materials. Friends and neigh-bors, professional associations, and some stores can provide references.

If you're contemplating major structural changes, an architect or de-signer can help you prepare plans, and a contractor can do the work. For re-pairs and any wall work you don't want to do yourself, turn to a subcontractor. Ask for bids and make comparisons— prices can vary widely.

Paint

For anyone who's ever seen a room almost magically transformed by paint, it's obvious why paint is such a popular wall covering. No other technique or material allows you to alter the look or mood of a room as quickly, economically, and easily as paint. And if you tire of the look in a few years, you can just as easily and inexpensively change it again.   Gain inspiration from the colorful photographs that follow. See how you can use paint to set a cheery, or perhaps a formal, mood; accent architectural features, such as moldings and trim; or create illusions, such as simulating marble or bringing the outdoors inside. You're limited only by your imagination.   Information about basic painting begins on page 32. This section introduces you to the paints and tools available today, tells you how to prepare the surface for painting, provides tips for handling a paintbrush and roller, and explains the proper painting sequence. The section on decorative painting, beginning on page 48, shows you how to create wonderfully striking effects, from subtle to sensational, with washes or glazes. Illustrated step-by-step directions for sponging, dragging, ragging, colorwashing, marbling, wood graining, and stenciling will help you achieve a truly unique finish.

Rich red walls form a dramatic backdrop for the impressive wood *tansu* and artistically arranged branches in this Oriental-style dining room. The white ceiling and casing provide a striking contrast.

PUTTING COLOR TO WORK

Indoors and outdoors flow together here: the blue-green of the living room walls mirrors the color of the bay beyond, and the contrasting white of the interior trim and ceiling is repeated on the veranda. Interior design: Ruth Livingston Interior Design.

A contrasting color on one wall breaks up the tall, narrow space of this stairwell and adds to its visual interest.

Understated light peach walls contribute to the open, airy feeling of this dining room. The white moldings and ceiling further brighten the room and make it seem more spacious. Interior design: Debra Coburn of House to Home.

Sophistication is supreme in this dining alcove, where the white ceiling and matching white trim and doors enhance the elegant taupe walls. The color motif appears again in the striped chair upholstery. Interior design: Robert W. Miller.

This bright, cheerful child's room features peachy pink walls. Echoing the colors of the furniture and drapes is the decorative, wall-mounted corner shelf unit, playfully painted yellow, green, and orange.

FANCIFUL FINISHES

Broken color embellishes a 1950s-style bathroom and complements the existing speckled tile. Three colors—mauve, beige, and gray—were sponged on the walls and then gently softened with cheesecloth. For the mirror frame and wall border, a beige glaze was applied over a black background, and then a pattern was created with crumpled paper. Interior design and decorative painting: Peggy Del Rosario.

An intriguing pattern and a three-dimensional effect were produced by ragrolling the wall. Pale beige with just a hint of salmon, the finish is subtle enough to serve as a splendid backdrop for almost any furnishings or ornamentation. Decorative painting: Claire Roman.

This rustic kitchen resembles a potting shed you might encounter in the Italian countryside. Coppery accents painted on the existing tile produce a verdigris effect. The walls, cabinets, door, and ceiling were aged and treated to look as if they had been carved out of stone. Interior design and decorative painting: Peggy Del Rosario.

Layers of earthy colors were built up on the walls in this bathroom, and then a final glaze was applied with stiff plastic. The fleur-de-lis pattern was stenciled with pewter metallic paint before the walls were varnished. A hand-painted star map covers the upper wall and ceiling. Decorative painting: Shelley Masters Studio.

Opulent furnishings demand an equally dramatic wall finish—and these vivid red walls, rag-rolled and varnished to resemble rich leather, are just the right touch. Interior design: David Stonesifer of Los Gatos Porch. Decorative painting: Claire Roman.

SPLENDID EFFECTS

Classic goes contemporary, as faux columns supporting a painted marble peak frame the windows in this spacious, modern living room. Interior design: Ann Jones, Interiors. Decorative painting: Adele Crawford, Painted Finishes.

Cleverly painted to look like marble, this elaborate crown molding adds a formal finishing touch to the room. Below, wall panels are covered with a blue-gray finish designed to look like stretched silk. Interior design: Charleen Matoza of La Fille du Roi Antiques & Interiors. Decorative painting: Tina Martinez of Furniture Art Studio.

A marble summit is the high point of this design, shown in a larger view on the facing page. Although flat, the painted structure—consisting of faux columns supporting a roof of painted stone and marble—appears to have depth and texture.

GRAND IMAGERY

Artistic inspiration comes naturally in this child's art room, which features furnishings decorated freehand. The abstract pattern on the lower walls, created by both sponging on and ragging on a blue glaze, sets off the creamy yellow paint on the upper walls and moldings. Decorative painting: Ann Blair Davison.

Romantic and playful, the treatment of this bathroom was inspired by 18th-century French flower paintings. The bewitching border, consisting of a ribbon and dangling, flower-filled basket, was painted freehand over a glazed background. Yellow, peach, and pink glazes were applied in irregular stripes over a white base so that the colors blend and the backdrop shows through. Interior design: Shelby de Quesada of Shelby Co. Decorative painting: Samantha Renko Design (border); Cathleen Ristow Lambridis of Chroma Designs (background).

A floral stencil helps bring the outdoors inside by echoing the greens, blues, and pinks in the flower garden visible through the window. Interior design and decorative painting: Cynthia Brian of Starstyle Interiors.

FLIGHTS OF FANTASY

This dreamy design features a vine-covered canopy twining to a cloud-painted ceiling. The wall murals present fanciful views of a French country garden. Interior design: Ledoux Design Associates and JoAnn Hirsch Kaleidoscope Designs. Decorative painting: Whimsey Walls and Deborah Brackman.

The crowning touch in this sumptuous study are intricately painted faux cornices complete with shadow patterns. The richly colored dragged walls impart the right note of formality, as well as complement the cream-colored cornices and moldings. Interior design: Cheryl Driver of Hilary Thatz, Inc. Decorative painting: David Mattice of Evans & Brown.

A collection of trompe l'oeil and real objects mingle playfully in a country-style setting. Only the candlestick, bird cage, and doll are real—the rest are painted-on pretenders. The fresh white plate rail and window and door trim contrast crisply with the soft, golden-glazed walls. Interior design: Osburn Design. Decorative painting: Iris Potter.

Basic Painting

Everyone, at one time or another, has done some painting. But using paint to transform a room involves more than just donning a pair of overalls and picking up a brush. For a successful job, it's essential to know how to select the right paint and painting tools, how to prepare the surface, and how best to apply the paint.

Everything you need to know about basic painting appears in this section. For the decorative painting techniques, turn to page 48. If you need help in choosing the right color for your walls, be sure to read the detailed information on color and design in the first chapter. Once you've decided on a particular color, try it out for a few days on a small section of your wall, looking at it in all different lights.

SHOPPING FOR PAINT

Although paint terminology and the profusion of brand names and grades can be overwhelming and confusing, a basic understanding of paint and how it works will help you decide on the right paint for the job.

Basically, paint is an opaque liquid that bonds to a surface and dries to a hard, durable finish. Pigment gives paint its color. Resins, or binders, surround the pigment particles to form a strong film that adheres to the surface. The pigment and resins are combined with a solvent—either water or petroleum distillates—to make the paint thin enough to be brushed or rolled on a surface.

The different types of paint each have their own unique qualities and specific uses. The most common types for interior surfaces are water-base, or latex, paints and oil-base, or alkyd, paints. Other paints are designed for special uses, such as covering acoustical panels or ceramic tiles. In addition, stains and clear finishes are available for wood surfaces.

Do your homework before going to the paint store. Make a list of the different surfaces you want to paint, their dimensions, and the type, color, and condition of the current finish.

You must decide on the new finish you want for each surface. Paint finishes range from flat, or mat, to high gloss. Since there's no industry standard for sheens, a medium gloss may be called pearl, satin, semigloss, or some other name, and it can range from moderately to quite shiny, depending on the manufacturer. A finish with a sheen is referred to as an enamel finish.

The glossier the finish, the more durable and washable it is. Glossy paint is used on woodwork as well as on kitchen, bathroom, and other surfaces exposed to grease or heavy wear. A flat or eggshell finish is suitable for light-duty surfaces, such as living room and bedroom walls and ceilings.

It doesn't pay to scrimp by buying an inferior or inappropriate coating. Although a good paint may cost nearly twice as much as the most inexpensive product, it covers in fewer coats and may require less frequent repainting. But don't choose a paint by price alone. Your best bet is to consult a reputable and knowledgeable paint dealer.

Always read the product label before buying the paint. It should tell you what surfaces the paint is designed for, how much area it will cover per gallon, what kind of surface prepara-

How Paint Is Changing

The paint you buy today is different from the paint you may have bought in the past. And paint will continue to change as manufacturers react to environmental concerns about it.

The main environmental problem is the volatile organic compound emissions from paint. These emissions result from the evaporation of thinner, also called solvent, into the air. Paint companies are responding by reducing the amount of thinner in their products.

Although thinners are found primarily in oil-base paints, they occur to some degree in water-base paints as well. When thinner is removed, it must be replaced with a nonvolatile oil or a resin. It's this reformulation process that's changing paint.

Modern oil-base paints, which are made of synthetic resins called alkyds instead of linseed or other natural oils, work like the old oil paints they replaced, but more effectively. Not only has thinner content been decreased, but also reduced are odor and toxic fumes, two

major problems with the old oil paints. Still, thinner is an essential component of alkyd paints.

Because the thinner content of latex paints is much less than that of alkyd paints, there's been a dramatic shift toward the water-base paints in recent years. They have fewer emission problems and are also easy to apply, dry quickly, and clean up with soap and water. Today, latex paints account for nearly 80 percent of all paint sold in the United States.

Air-quality control standards vary from state to state, and even from city to city. In areas where the standards are particularly stringent, certain oil-base products either are no longer available or are available only in quarts instead of gallon cans.

All of this doesn't mean that oil-base paints will be banned in the future. More likely, environmental rules will force paint companies to continue reformulating products to meet increasingly strict standards.

Interior Paints for All Surfaces

Surface	Prime or First Coat	Finish Coat(s)	Comments
New wallboard	Seal surface with PVA (polyvinyl acetate) sealer; let dry thoroughly.	Apply two coats of latex or alkyd flat or enamel paint. Sand lightly between enamel coats.	Don't use an alkyd primer—it will raise nap in paper.
New plaster	Seal surface with a vinyl acrylic wall primer; let dry thoroughly.	Apply two coats of latex or alkyd flat or enamel paint. Sand lightly between enamel coats.	You can use PVA sealer instead of vinyl acrylic wall primer, but you'll need more to do the same job.
Existing wallboard or plaster	Treat small stains with a white-pigmented shellac, larger ones with a quick-drying alkyd primer. Spot-prime patches with PVA sealer or finish paint diluted 10 percent. If surface is more than 5 years old or there's a big color change, prime entire surface, using a vinyl acrylic wall primer over a latex finish, an alkyd primer over an oil-base finish.	Apply two coats of latex or alkyd flat or enamel paint. Sand lightly between enamel coats.	When applying an enamel finish over an existing flat finish, ensure uniform sheen by priming entire surface.
Bare wood to be painted	Use an alkyd enamel undercoater. (On fir, you can use a latex enamel undercoater since it doesn't bleed.) Let dry overnight.	Apply a first coat of latex or alkyd enamel paint thinned 10 percent with appropriate solvent (water for latex and paint thinner for alkyd); let dry thoroughly. Sand lightly; then apply a second, undiluted coat.	An enamel finish is usually recommended for wood.
Painted wood to be repainted	Chip away loose, flaking paint and sand smooth. Spot-prime bare wood spots with a white-pigmented shellac; let dry for 30 minutes.	Apply a first coat of undiluted latex or alkyd enamel paint; let dry thoroughly. Sand lightly; then apply a second coat and let dry overnight.	An enamel finish is usually recommended for wood.
Bare wood to be stained	Fill holes with natural latex wood patch before staining. For uniform stain absorption on soft woods, use a stain-controlling sealer. Stain in desired color; let dry overnight. If surface feels rough, apply a quick-drying sanding sealer and sand lightly.	Apply a first coat of varnish thinned 10 percent with paint thinner; let dry thoroughly. Sand lightly; then apply a second, undiluted coat and let dry for 24 hours.	Polyurethane or other clear finishes can be applied over a stain and some sanding sealers; see manufacturer's directions.
Bare wood to be coated with a clear finish	Apply varnish, polyurethane, or other clear finish in desired sheen.	Apply one or two additional coats of clear finish, sanding lightly between coats.	Test coating on an inconspicuous spot. Thin first coat, if necessary, for easier application (see label).
Masonry	Use acrylic or latex block filler. For a waterproof surface, follow with a hydrostatic coating; if it's going over a previous coating, consult a dealer—all coatings aren't compatible.	Apply two coats of latex or alkyd flat or enamel paint. Sand lightly between enamel coats.	Remove any powdery crust. Wash with muriatic acid, rinse thoroughly, and let dry for 72 hours.
Metal	Remove dirt with vinegar; rinse. Sand off rust; prime. Use rust-inhibitive primer on new metal that will rust, latex metal primer on galvanized metal, conventional metal primer on aluminum.	Apply two coats of latex or alkyd enamel in desired sheen or colored polyurethane. Don't sand between coats.	Flat wall paint isn't recommended.

tion is necessary, what the appropriate primer is, and what safety precautions need to be taken. To estimate how much paint to buy, see at right.

Latex paints

Synonymous with water-base paint, latex accounts for the vast majority of house paint sold today, and for good reason. Because water is the solvent, latex paints dry quickly, usually in a little more than an hour, although a full cure of a latex enamel can take about two weeks. Also, latex paints are practically odorless. Best of all, you can clean up with soap and water.

When you apply a flat latex wall paint, you can stop in the middle of a wall, start later, and never see where you left off—although that's not the recommended way to paint; regardless of the type of paint you're using, it's always better to finish a surface from one corner to the other before stopping.

Surface preparation is extremely important to the bonding of a latex paint. If the walls aren't clean and properly primed, latex paint can easily peel and crack.

Although today's latex high-gloss finishes are as shiny as alkyd ones, they're not as durable. Also, unlike an alkyd finish, latex tears or melts to a gummy consistency when you try to sand it.

Flat latex paint is the most common wall and ceiling paint. Latex enamel finishes are used for woodwork and sometimes for other surfaces where greater washability is desired.

You can tell latex quality by the type of resin used. The highest-quality and most durable latex paint is one containing 100 percent acrylic resin. Vinyl acrylic and other blends are next in quality. A latex paint containing solely vinyl resin is the least durable and poorest-quality latex.

Alkyd paints

These modern-day oil-base house paints, made of synthetic resins, have largely replaced paints containing linseed and other natural oils. Alkyds are more durable than latex paints and generally level out better, drying virtually

Estimating for Paint

To figure out how much paint to buy, you must know the square footage of the area you intend to paint, as well as the paint's spreading rate—the surface area that a can of paint will cover. Most paints have a spreading rate of about 400 square feet per gallon; for the exact figure, read the label on the can of paint you're buying.

To determine square footage, measure the width of each wall, add the figures together, and then multiply the total by the room's height. For example, if the room measures 16 by 20 feet and is 8 feet tall, the square footage of the walls is 576 square feet (16 + 16 + 20 + 20 x 8 = 576). For the ceiling, multiply the width by the length.

Next, estimate how much of the area contains surfaces that won't be painted, such as a fireplace, windows, wallpaper, and areas you'll paint separately, such as woodwork. If those surfaces account for more than 10 percent of the room, deduct the amount from your total.

To figure out how many cans of paint you'll need, divide the total square footage by the spreading rate of the paint and round up to the next whole number. For example, if the spreading rate of the paint is 400 feet per gallon, for the walls of the room described earlier you'll need to buy two 1-gallon cans (576 ÷ 400 = 1.44, rounded up to 2). Remember to double your requirement if you're applying two coats.

You can calculate the amount of trim paint required by measuring trim areas separately. Or, like professional painters, you can figure on about a quarter as much trim paint as wall paint.

free of brush marks. They have "bite," a sticking quality not inherent in latex. You can easily sand an alkyd surface—a critical factor if you're applying successive enamel coats.

On the other hand, alkyds are harder to apply, tend to sag more, and take longer to dry. Also, you need to keep a wet edge when you use alkyds; if you stop in the middle of a surface and resume later, the areas will look different when they dry. Alkyds require cleanup with paint thinner.

In some areas, flat alkyd is either not available or sold only in quarts. Alkyd enamel finishes are most often used for woodwork, and sometimes for painting walls and ceilings where a high degree of durability is important, such as in kitchens and bathrooms.

Today, alkyd paints don't smell as much as they used to, since many of the thinners, or solvents, have been removed. Most of the problems with odor and fumes occur when you add large amounts of paint thinner to the paint, as when making an oil glaze (see page 49). If you can't ventilate the area sufficiently, wear a respirator.

Special paints

Latex and alkyd paints don't work on certain surfaces, such as acoustical panels, tile, and glass. For these, you'll have to use special paint.

■ *Acoustical ceiling paint.* A water-base porous flat paint that doesn't change the sound-deadening qualities of the panels as ordinary paint does, acoustical ceiling paint is available in only a few colors. It's usually applied with a sprayer or a special roller and dries quickly to a flat finish.

■ *Epoxy.* Epoxy is the best—and sometimes the only—paint to use on hard, impermeable surfaces, such as ceramic tile, plastic, porcelain, fiberglass, and glass. Usually available in semigloss and high gloss, epoxy can be scrubbed and is resistant to abrasion. It should be sprayed on the surface, since it dries so fast that it's difficult to brush on without leaving marks.

To make the epoxy paint adhere better, apply a primer-bonder formulated for use on nonporous surfaces.

■ *Texture paint.* The main use of thick texture paint is to disguise wall defects. Add a texture paint to a flat wall paint and then brush it on a small area at a time. While the paint is wet, create a rough textured finish with a trowel, putty knife, sponge, paint roller, or other implement.

Premixed latex texture paints are used for light stipple patterns. Powder textures, which come in large bags and must be mixed with water, are used for heavier adobe or stucco finishes.

Wood stains

Since most stains are made for a particular effect or condition, it's best to discuss the job with your paint dealer before choosing a product. Stains are available with a base of alkyd, linseed oil, or water and with varying amounts of pigment.

Pigmented, or dye-colored, wiping stain is among the most commonly used. You simply apply it with a brush or rag, wait for a while, and then wipe it off. If the surface feels rough, use a clear, quick-drying sanding sealer; then sand the finish smooth.

Clear finishes

Polyurethane, varnish, shellac, and some new clear, nonyellowing water-base coatings are among the finishes used to cover bare or stained wood so the grain shows through. Most come in a range of finishes from mat to glossy. Some, like polyurethane, are also available in colors.

■ *Polyurethane.* Apply polyurethane plastic coating to cabinets and wood paneling when extreme durability is required. Penetrating resin sealer, a type of polyurethane that soaks into the wood instead of coating the surface, should be used when you want to maintain the wood's texture. Use paint thinner for thinning and cleanup.

■ *Varnishes.* Although durable, varnishes aren't as tough as polyurethane. Ask your paint dealer for the best type for your job. Use paint thinner for thinning and cleanup.

■ *Shellac.* Apply shellac, which comes in orange or white (clear), only over bare or stained wood—its alcohol content could dissolve other coatings. It isn't recommended for kitchens, bathrooms, and other areas exposed to moisture; water causes spotting on the finish. Virtually any brush marks that appear when shellac is first applied aren't visible when it's dry. Use denatured alcohol for thinning and cleanup.

■ *Water-base transparent coatings.* Some transparent coatings, including nonyellowing types, can be used on bare or stained wood as well as on all painted surfaces. For more on these coatings, see page 48.

Primers

You need a primer when the surface you intend to paint is porous or is incompatible with the finish paint. An existing painted surface in good condition and compatible with the finish coat is already primed and may not need an additional primer. Consult your paint dealer to be sure.

Several types of priming agents are available for interior surfaces. A *primer,* which has no shine, is generally used under a flat finish. A *primer-sealer* is a type of latex primer used on new wallboard; it's usually sold as PVA, or polyvinyl acetate, sealer. An *undercoater* is a type of priming agent formulated

Painting Terms

Acrylic paint. Latex paint containing all acrylic resin.

Alkyd paint. Modern oil-base paint containing synthetic resins called alkyds. This paint has replaced oil paints containing linseed and other natural oils.

Cutting in. Painting a narrow band along the edges of an area with a brush before rolling on paint.

Enamel. A finishing material with very fine pigments that produces a smooth, hard, lustrous finish.

Epoxy. An extremely durable, plastic-like paint used on nonporous surfaces.

Gloss. The degree of shininess of a paint finish. The higher the gloss, the more durable and long-lasting the finish will be.

Latex paint. Water-base paint containing acrylic resin, vinyl resin, or a blend.

Polyurethane. A resin; also the plastic coating made from the resin.

Primer. A first coat (usually a special paint) applied to help a finish coat adhere to the surface. The primer may be water base or oil base.

Resins. Chemicals that hold together the ingredients in paint; sometimes called binders.

Shellac. A coating made from a resinous material called lac and used as a clear sealer or finish.

Thinners. Volatile liquids used to regulate the consistency of paint and other finishes; also sold as paint thinner or mineral spirits for cleanup of alkyds.

Varnish. A liquid coating that converts to a translucent or transparent solid film after application.

Vinyl. A class of resins found in some types of latex paint and in various specialized coatings.

Wallboard. A wall material applied in large sheets or panels; also known as drywall, gypsum board, and plasterboard.

for use under an enamel finish; it can also be used under a flat finish.

You can purchase either a latex or an alkyd primer or undercoater. Although either type of primer or undercoater can be used under a latex or alkyd finish, it's best to use an alkyd priming agent under an alkyd finish, except on new wallboard, where it will raise the nap on the paper.

Either type of priming agent will do a good job under a latex finish, but most people opt for a latex primer or undercoater, since it's easy to use, dries quickly, and cleans up with soap and water—just as latex paint does. For more information on primers and priming, see page 40.

SELECTING & USING TOOLS

Even the best paint can produce disappointing results if you don't have the right equipment. (For a look at some basic preparation and painting tools, see the facing page.) Good-quality tools suited to the task and used the right way will give you a professional-looking paint job.

The tools you'll need to prep the walls—a paint scraper, putty knife, abrasive cleaner, and so on—are discussed in the following section (see page 38). For painting, several high-quality brushes and a good roller are essential.

Brushes

Natural bristle brushes are traditionally used to apply alkyd paint and other finishes that clean up in paint thinner. Don't use them for applying latex paint and other water-base products, because the bristles become limp when they soak up water.

Useful painting tools include (1) bucket with roller grid, (2) caulking gun with caulking compound, (3) masking tape, (4) sandpaper and sanding block, (5) painter's mitt, (6) paint roller with extension pole, (7) pad applicator, (8) straight-edged brush, (9) angled sash brush, (10) trim brush, (11) tack cloth, (12) edge guide, (13) paint scraper, (14) foam brushes, (15) wire brush, (16) putty knives.

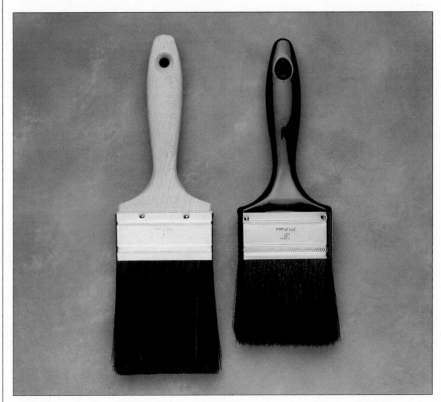

Superior-quality brush (at left) has long, flagged bristles firmly set into an easy-to-grip wood handle. On less expensive brush (at right), connection isn't as secure, bristles are short and splayed, and plastic handle may become slippery during use.

Choose a synthetic filament brush for latex paint. Polyester brushes stay sturdy in water, keeping their shape for detail work. A good-quality synthetic brush can also be used with alkyd paint.

You can get by nicely with three brushes: a 2-inch trim brush, a 1½-inch angled sash brush, and a 3-inch straight-edged brush. Although professional painters generally use a 4-inch brush because it allows them to apply more paint faster, you'll probably find the 3-inch brush easier to handle.

Good-quality brushes perform very differently from less expensive ones. A good brush is well balanced, holds a lot of paint, and puts the paint where you want it. For an illustration of what to look for, compare the brushes pictured above.

Inspect any brush carefully before you buy it. Grip it as if you were painting. It should feel comfortable in your hand—not so awkward or heavy that using it tires you.

Fan out the bristles and check for flags, or split ends. The more flags there are, the more paint the brush can hold. Most of the bristles should be long, but there should be some short bristles mixed among the longer ones.

The bristles should be thick, flexible, and tapered so that they're thicker at the base than at the tip, and they should be set firmly into the handle with epoxy cement, not glue.

Paint rollers

Look for a roller with a heavy-gauge steel frame, an expandable wire sleeve, a good-quality cover, and a comfortable handle threaded with a metal sleeve to accommodate an extension pole. A 9-inch roller will handle nearly all jobs.

For some work you may need a special roller: a trim roller for trim and window sashes; a beveled corner roller for corners, ceiling borders, and paneling grooves; and a roller made of grooved foam for acoustical surfaces.

When you're buying a standard roller, choose an appropriate cover for the paint you're using. With latex paint, you'll want a nylon cover. Nylon and wool blend, lambskin, and mohair covers are recommended for alkyd paint. Nap thickness on roller covers varies from 1/16 inch to 1 1/4 inches. The smoother the surface you're painting, the shorter the nap you'll need.

A 3- to 4-foot extension pole allows you to reach high walls and ceilings, in many cases eliminating the need for ladders or scaffolding. Leave the extension pole on when you're painting low areas to avoid stooping.

Rolling from a 5-gallon bucket equipped with a roller grid is faster and neater than using a roller tray. Don't bother with a roller shield, a device intended to minimize spattering. Spatter is due to excessive speed in rolling and to improper roller nap thickness. Inexpensive paints also tend to spatter more than good-quality paints.

Other paint applicators

Disposable foam brushes are handy for small jobs or quick touchups. A pad applicator with a replaceable pad is useful for painting corners and edges. As with roller covers made of the same materials, nylon pads are used with latex paints; nylon and wool blend, lambskin, and mohair pads are recommended for alkyds.

A painter's mitt is ideal for painting irregular or contoured surfaces, such as pipes, grilles, and radiators. You dip the mitt into the paint and rub the paint onto the surface.

PREPARING THE SURFACE

A good paint job may require three or four hours of preparation for every hour spent painting. Preparation consists of organizing the room, scraping, making repairs, sanding, cleaning, masking, and priming.

Organizing the room

Move all lightweight furniture and accessories out of the room. Push heavy furniture into the middle of the room and cover it with drop cloths. Remove everything you can from the walls. Unscrew heating and air-conditioning duct covers.

After turning off the power to the room, remove electrical faceplates and any fixtures. Tie a plastic garbage bag around a light fixture if you can't take it down, as shown on page 45. Try to loosen the plate before shielding it.

It's best to remove knobs, handles, and locks from doors, windows, and cabinets. Identify all pieces (write on masking tape attached to the item) so you can replace them correctly later.

Protect the flooring with canvas drop cloths, which, unlike plastic sheeting, absorb paint. When you walk on plastic, you can slip on the paint or pick it up on the soles of your shoes and track it around.

Scraping

Older homes especially may have chipped or peeling paint that will have to be scraped off interior surfaces. The trick is to scrape hard enough to get off the old paint, but not so hard that you dig into the surface.

The best scrapers are those with edges that can be sharpened with a metal file. A hook blade scraper does a fast job on large areas; a broad knife is more convenient for small areas. A wire brush can handle light flaking.

Sometimes, the old finish is in such bad condition that the paint must be removed entirely. The easiest way to strip old paint is with a commercial liquid paint remover. Follow the application directions on the container. Then scrape off the softened paint. Finally, sand the surface lightly until it's clean and smooth.

Although you can sometimes paint over wallpaper, it's best to remove it, especially if it's tearing or flaking (for directions, see page 77). After all the adhesive is removed, wash the wall with an abrasive cleaner, rinse well, and let the surface dry for 24 hours.

Making repairs

Carefully inspect the area you're painting for holes, cracks, and other minor damage. You'll be able to fix most surface damage yourself, though you may have to call in a professional to repair very large holes or cracks. If you can insert the tip of your little finger into a crack, you should have your foundation inspected.

To keep patched areas from showing through later, spot-prime them with PVA sealer or with your finish paint diluted 10 percent.

Holes in plaster over lath. Knock out the loose plaster with a wire brush and an old screwdriver. Clean out the plaster in and behind the lath to pro-

■ PATCHING HOLES IN PLASTER OVER LATH

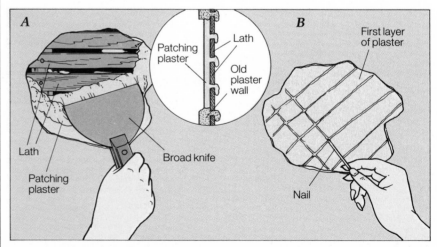

For holes larger than 2 inches across, use a broad knife to apply a thin layer of patching plaster, working from outer edges toward center (A). Score with a nail (B), let dry, and fill with two more layers of patching plaster.

■ PATCHING HOLES WITH NO BACKING

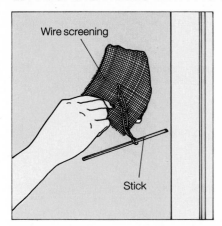

To patch a hole 4 inches or less in diameter, wire a stick to a piece of wire screening slightly larger than hole. Insert screening.

Draw screening to back of wall by rolling up wire on stick. Fill hole halfway, cut wire flush with surface, and finish filling.

vide a clean surface to which the new plaster can adhere. Brush the area clean and dampen it with a sponge for better adhesion.

If the hole is smaller than 2 inches across, fill it with one layer of patching plaster. For larger holes, use three layers. Working from the outer edges toward the middle, fill about one-third the depth of the patch, making sure to get plaster behind the lath (see illustration on facing page). Score this first layer with a nail and let it dry.

Redampen the area; then apply a second layer to two-thirds the depth of the patch. After this layer is dry, finish

filling the hole. Sand it smooth and spot-prime.

Small holes and cracks. Fill nail holes with ready-mix spackling compound. Before patching other small holes and cracks, brush them clean, dampen the surface or apply a sealer, and let the surface dry. Using a flexible, narrow-bladed putty knife, fill the holes with spackling compound, wood filler, or patching plaster. After patching any area, smooth it and spot-prime.

Woodwork may have "checking"—small cracks caused by the expansion and contraction of wood as it

ages—that must be fixed before you repaint. Sand the damaged area down to bare wood; then apply an enamel undercoater and let it dry thoroughly. After filling the cracks with spackling compound or wood filler, prime the area again.

Holes with no backing. To repair a hole no larger than 4 inches across in plaster or wallboard, clean it and cut a piece of wire screening slightly larger than the hole. Tie one end of a piece of wire to the center of the screening and the other end to a 6-inch stick, as shown at left. Push the screening through the hole; then draw the screening tightly to the back of the wall by rolling the wire up on the stick.

Dampen the area and fill the hole to half its depth, using patching plaster on a plaster surface and joint compound on a wallboard surface. (The powder form of joint compound will dry faster than the ready-mix type.) After the patching compound is dry, cut the wire level with the top and redampen the patch. Fill the hole flush with the wall. Allow it to dry; then sand it smooth and spot-prime.

An alternative method is to fix the hole with a prefabricated self-adhesive patch, but the wall won't be as smooth.

Large holes in wallboard. Cut a neat rectangle around the hole (see drawing below, at left) with a sharp

■ REPAIRING LARGE HOLES IN WALLBOARD

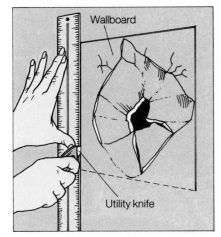

Cut a neat rectangle around hole. Measure opening and then cut a patch 1 inch wider all around from a new piece of wallboard.

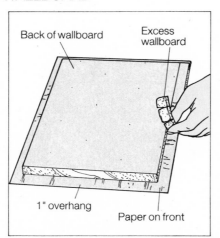

Place patch right side down. Cut a plug that matches opening without scoring front paper. Lift off excess, leaving overhang.

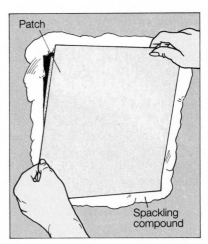

Spread spackling compound around edges of hole, place patch in hole, and coat edges and surface with more compound.

utility knife or hacksaw blade. From another piece of wallboard, cut a patch 1 inch wider on all sides than the rectangle you've just cut.

Laying the new piece of wallboard right side down, cut a plug the same size as the wall rectangle, but without scoring the paper on the front surface of the wallboard. Lift off the 1 inch of cut board around the plug from the front paper, leaving a 1-inch margin of paper on all four sides.

Spread a thin layer of spackling compound around the hole and on its edges. Position the patch and press it into the hole until it's flush with the wall surface. Cover the seams and the entire surface with spackling compound. After it's dry, sand it smooth and spot-prime.

Medium-size wall or ceiling cracks.
As long as the crack isn't big enough to accommodate the tip of your little finger, you can usually fix it yourself.

Because a house continually expands and contracts, a crack filled with a rigid material won't stay fixed for long. Instead, you need to apply a pregummed mesh tape and a flexible patching compound. The tape will reinforce the crack and help hold the patching compound. Both materials will give with the movement of the house, keeping the crack from redeveloping under normal circumstances.

The repair will only be effective if you clean out the crack thoroughly. Use a crack opener, available at paint stores, to dig out loose material; then vacuum. Tape the crack and apply patching compound thinly so that it just conceals the tape. If necessary, apply another thin coat to hide the edges of the tape. Sand lightly before spot-priming.

Joint separations.
Seal minor gaps between window frames, moldings, and other trim and the wall surface with caulking compound applied with a caulking gun. Check the label to make sure you can paint over the caulk.

Apply a bead of caulk along the joint or crack; then run your finger or a putty knife along it and press it in. Fill deep cracks in stages, giving each layer time to dry. Since dry caulk doesn't sand well, remove excess caulk with a damp rag as you work. You don't need to spot-prime caulk.

Water-damaged areas.
Sometimes, moisture penetrates a wall, flaking and staining paint and rotting wood. Before making any repairs to the damaged surface, you must find and get rid of the source of moisture.

If there's any rotted wood, cut it out and replace it. Remove the old paint completely with a liquid paint remover. Allow the surface to dry for several days; then, to seal it, apply a white-pigmented shellac or, for larger areas, a quick-drying alkyd primer.

Sanding

One reason to sand a surface is to smooth it. If the old finish is flaking or peeling, you must lightly sand it before applying a new coat. You also need to sand patched areas and rough bare wood before painting.

Another reason to sand is to rough up a gloss before you paint on top of it. Sanding gives the finish "bite" so that the new paint will adhere. You can use sandpaper, a liquid deglosser or sander, or an abrasive cleaner, such as trisodium phosphate (TSP).

If you're using sandpaper on a surface with a very high sheen, begin with coarse sandpaper and finish with a fine-grit paper. A liquid deglosser is convenient for hard-to-sand areas and for removing floor wax from baseboards. An abrasive cleaner acts as a deglosser, but only if a light sanding is needed.

Be sure to wear rubber gloves when using a liquid deglosser or an abrasive cleaner, and don't forget to rinse the wall after using the cleaner.

Cleaning

After vacuuming the room, use a tack cloth to dust all the surfaces that will be painted. Then wash them with an abrasive cleaner and rinse well. For very greasy spots, sponge on paint thinner, blot dry, and wash with the cleaner.

In mildewed areas, it's not enough simply to wash the surface. To kill the mildew spores, scrub the walls with liquid bleach or with a solution of half bleach and half water. Then wash with an abrasive cleaner and rinse thoroughly. Allow all washed surfaces to dry for 24 hours.

Periodic cleaning of painted surfaces can reduce the need for frequent repainting. An annual cleaning with water and a mild detergent will prolong the life of most paints.

Masking

If you have a steady hand and lots of experience painting, you may not need masking tape. But most people find it helpful for protecting surfaces that could get spattered and for keeping a crisp delineation between two types or colors of paint.

It's important to have the right masking tape. If you're using a brush against the tape, use the kind with good adhesion for a tight edge, rather than all-purpose tape. That way, you won't have a problem with paint seeping behind the tape.

There's a kind of masking tape that can be fastened to delicate surfaces, such as wallpaper or a newly painted wall, without causing any damage. Another kind of masking tape can stay on for a long period of time without leaving any residue when it's removed.

Priming

Most paints are designed to be used over some type of priming agent. It often isn't necessary to prime an existing finish that's in good condition, but if you don't know whether the old finish is compatible with your new one, apply an alkyd primer. (For more information about priming, see the chart on page 33.) Don't forget to rough up a glossy surface by sanding it, whether you're priming it or painting directly on top of it.

Your primer coat should cover the area completely but doesn't have to be as neat as the finish coat. Use a brush or roller to apply the primer.

You'll need to use a primer in the following situations:

■ **Bare wood to be painted with an alkyd or latex enamel finish.** Use an alkyd enamel undercoater. (A latex enamel undercoater can be used on fir.)

■ *New wallboard surface.* Use PVA (polyvinyl acetate) sealer.

■ *New plaster surface.* Use a vinyl acrylic wall primer.

■ *Patched areas.* Spot-prime with PVA sealer; or use finish paint diluted 10 percent.

■ *Stained areas.* Spot-prime with a white-pigmented shellac or a quick-drying alkyd primer. (The shellac is preferred, but it's too brittle to be applied over large areas.)

■ *Unpainted metal.* Apply a rust-inhibitive primer (each metal has its own primer).

■ *Rough, coarse, or porous masonry.* Use block filler, a penetrating coating that fills holes in masonry.

■ *Drastic color change between existing paint and a new finish.* Use a tinted primer or undercoater; then apply two finish coats.

PAINTING

The best way to avoid painting yourself into a corner, spattering paint onto newly painted surfaces, or inadver-tently touching a just-painted edge is to follow a painting sequence. First, apply any stains or clear finishes to woodwork. Next, paint the ceiling. Then paint the walls, starting from the top and working your way down. Finally, brush paint on woodwork—first the moldings and then the windows, doors, and cabinets.

When you apply two coats of glossy paint, as is often the case when you paint woodwork, ensure a good bond by sanding lightly between coats and wiping with a tack cloth.

Use a roller wherever you can—rolling on paint is much easier and faster than brushing it on. Use a brush to cut in areas that will be rolled and to paint woodwork. (How to cut in is explained at right. For illustrations on painting with a brush and a roller, see pages 42–43.)

When you apply paint with a brush, never work directly from the paint can if you can help it. Pour paint into a bucket and stir it. You may want to "box" the paint, that is, mix paint from two or more cans into a bucket in order to eliminate slight color differences among cans.

Get the right amount of paint on the brush by dipping it into the paint and slapping it against the inside of the bucket; don't wipe the brush against the rim. Paint with the full face of the brush and not just the tip.

Before you dip a roller into paint, wet the cover in the appropriate solvent (water for latex and paint thinner for alkyd) to prime it and to get rid of any lint. Be sure to squeeze out excess solvent to prevent any drips and to avoid diluting the paint.

Then dip the roller into the paint. You can use a roller tray as your paint reservoir, but it's easier to load up your roller from a 5-gallon bucket equipped with a roller grid. Rolling back and forth along the grid will control the amount of paint on the roller.

When you're working overhead, carry less paint on your brush or roller, and wear goggles to protect your eyes. Also wear a hat—you'll quickly discover why hats are so popular among professional painters.

Cutting in with a brush

When you cut in, you're using a brush to paint a border along the edges and corners of a surface and around any fixtures or trim, as shown in the illustrations below. The space within the

■ CUTTING IN WITH A BRUSH

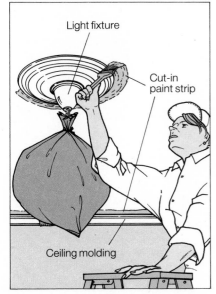

To cut in a ceiling, brush on paint above molding or ceiling line and around any light fixtures.

To cut in a wall, brush on paint below molding or ceiling line, above baseboard, and around frames of doors and windows.

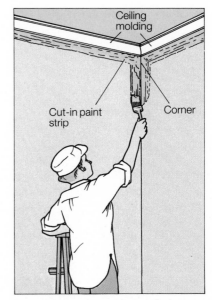

To cut in a wall corner, use a brush to paint joint and a 2-inch or wider strip on either side of corner.

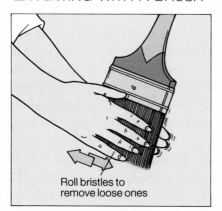

1 Roll bristle ends between your palms to remove loose bristles; shake brush vigorously. If you moisten bristles first (use water for latex paint and paint thinner for alkyd), be sure to wipe off any excess moisture to prevent drips.

Dip brush half the length of bristles

2 Stir paint thoroughly while it's still in can. Then pour paint into a clean, rimless bucket until bucket is half-full. Dip brush half the length of its bristles into paint two or three times to saturate bristles thoroughly.

Stir gently to spread bristles

3 Dip brush a third to half the length of its bristles into paint in bucket; then gently stir paint with brush to spread bristles slightly. (Stir paint with brush only after first saturating bristles and not on subsequent dippings.)

Slap brush gently 2 or 3 times

4 Lift brush straight up, letting excess paint drip into bucket. Gently slap both sides of brush against inside of bucket two or three times. Don't wipe brush across lip of bucket or bristles may separate into clumps, leaving less paint on brush.

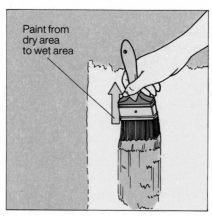

Paint from dry area to wet area

5 Spread paint smoothly and evenly over a 3-foot area, gradually reducing pressure at end of stroke. Paint from a dry area to a wet edge. On smooth surfaces, direct final strokes one way; on rough ones, vary direction; on wood, paint parallel to grain.

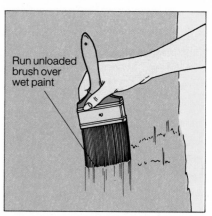

Run unloaded brush over wet paint

6 When area is filled, blend brush marks by running unloaded brush very lightly over wet paint. Begin next area a few inches away from last finished area. When new area is completed, brush into previously finished area, blending overlap.

borders will be filled in later with a paint roller.

With flat latex paint, you can cut in entire surfaces before rolling, and you won't have a problem with the brushed areas and the rolled areas looking different when they dry. With latex enamel or any alkyd, it's better to cut in small areas at a time and roll before the cut-in section dries. Always be sure to keep a wet edge; otherwise the overlapped areas will look inconsistent when they dry.

Where the ceiling meets the walls is the first area to cut in. If you're using the same color and type of paint for the ceiling and walls, you can paint the joint and several inches out on each side. If there's crown molding, cut in on either side of it.

If you're using a different color or type of paint on the ceiling, cut in and roll the whole ceiling before you tackle the walls. Don't forget to paint around any light fixtures when you cut in the ceiling.

Then cut in along the top and bottom edges of the walls and in the corners. Paint at least 2 inches out from the corners in both directions. Also cut in around the doors, windows, and any wall fixtures.

Finishing up with a roller

There are three parts to rolling: first, you roll paint onto a section; then you roll in various directions to even out the paint; finally, you roll lightly in long strokes to get rid of roller marks. Always roll slowly to avoid spattering.

To paint a ceiling, roll on paint in rectangles approximately 2 by 3 feet, starting in a corner and working across the short dimension of the ceiling. In

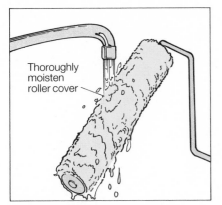

1 After placing roller cover on frame, moisten cover thoroughly with appropriate solvent (water for latex and paint thinner for alkyd) to get rid of any lint. Squeeze out excess solvent or blot cover with a clean, dry, lint-free cloth.

2 Dip roller into 1 to 2 gallons of paint poured into a 5-gallon bucket. (You can use a roller tray instead, but a large bucket is more convenient.) To control amount of paint on roller, run roller back and forth on grid positioned in bucket.

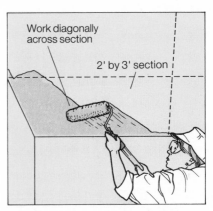

3 Paint ceiling first. Do a small section (about 2 by 3 feet) at a time, starting in a corner and going across shorter dimension. Apply paint diagonally; then roll back and forth to distribute evenly. Reload roller often and roll slowly to avoid spatters.

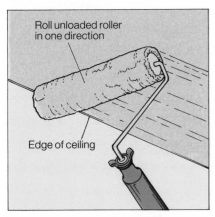

4 Roll as close to edges of ceiling as possible to cover any textural differences between brush marks made when cutting in and roller marks. For final strokes on ceiling, lightly roll unloaded roller across each section in one direction.

5 Next, roll walls. Starting in an upper corner of wall and working from top to bottom, apply paint thickly in a series of big Ws. Then backtrack and fill in Ws, rolling in different directions to fill in shapes. Roll slowly to avoid spatters.

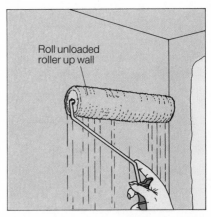

6 Apply paint close to edges and corners of wall to conceal differences between brush marks made when cutting in and roller marks. Finish by rolling unloaded roller across wall in one direction, working from bottom to top.

each rectangle, roll on paint diagonally and then distribute it evenly with horizontal and vertical strokes. Overlap brush marks made when cutting in. Keep your finishing strokes light and roll in one direction only.

The easiest way to cover a wall is to roll paint on thickly in a series of big Ws. Start at an upper corner and work from top to bottom. Then backtrack and fill in the Ws, distributing the paint evenly by rolling in various directions. Finally, roll the unloaded roller vertically from bottom to top across the entire wall.

Painting moldings

For best results, use a 1½-inch angled sash brush to paint narrow moldings and a 2-inch trim brush on wider ones.

Brush paint along the length of the molding; then brush in the opposite direction, if possible, to spread the paint evenly. Finally, brush lightly along the length to obscure the brush strokes.

Begin with the moldings closest to the ceiling and work down. Brush paint on smoothly and evenly, covering any caulking. A flexible edge guide allows you to paint the baseboard below the

carpet line (see page 45). For wide baseboards, first paint the top and bottom edges with a narrow brush; then paint the vertical surface with a wider brush.

Painting windows

A steady hand is the best tool for painting the wood parts of windows. The right brush—an angled sash brush that reaches neatly into corners—is also important. Load the brush lightly.

Resist the temptation to do a fast paint job, thinking you'll scrape off excess paint later; scraping can permanently scratch the glass. Instead, cover the edges of the glass with masking tape. Don't leave tape on windows in the sun, since it may bond to the glass.

Let the paint slightly overlap the glass. This will seal the finish to the glass, so that any condensation forming on the glass won't get under the paint and cause peeling.

Double-hung windows. If the sashes are removable, lift them out, lay them on a table, and paint them. Be prepared to leave the sashes out long enough to dry thoroughly.

If the sashes aren't removable, you'll need to raise and lower them as needed to reach all parts of the window. (For a look at the parts of a double-hung window, see the drawing at right.) Paint the outer, or upper, sash first. If the windows have small panes, begin with the horizontal muntins and then work on the vertical ones. Next, paint the exposed parts of the stiles, the top rail, and the bottom rail, in that order. Then paint the inner, or lower, sash, starting with the muntins and finishing with the rails.

To prevent sticking, carefully move the sashes once or twice while the paint is drying.

To paint the trim around a double-hung window, begin with the head cas-

■ ANATOMY OF A DOUBLE-HUNG WINDOW

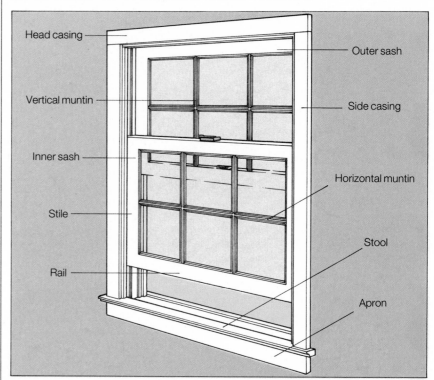

ing; then paint down the sides. Next, paint the stool, finishing with the apron.

Finally, you need to wax a wood jamb (the vertical track where the window slides). Don't wax a metal jamb and don't paint any jamb, since that can

result in the window's sticking to the jambs later.

Casement windows. First, paint any vertical muntins and then any horizontal ones. Next, paint the top rails, the bottom rails, and the stiles. Finally, paint the casing.

Painting doors

The painting sequence is exactly the same whether you paint a door on or off its hinges.

To remove a door, slip the hinge pins out, but don't unscrew the hinges themselves. Lean the door against a wall with two small blocks under the bottom edge and a third wedge between the top edge and the wall. Or lay the door across sawhorses; don't apply too much paint or it may puddle.

Always paint a door from top to bottom. For flat doors, roll on the paint and then brush it out smoothly in the direction of the grain. For doors with inset panels, as shown at left, first paint the panel moldings and the recesses of the panels. Then paint the panels. Finally, paint the horizontal and then the

■ PAINTING DOORS

On a door with inset panels, paint, in order, panel moldings, recesses, panels, and horizontal and vertical strips.

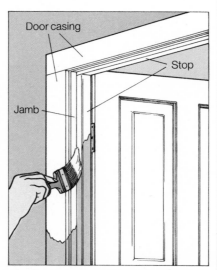

If door opens away from room, paint jamb and two surfaces of stop. If door opens into room, paint jamb and door side of stop.

Tricks of the Trade

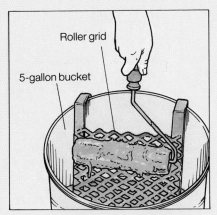

A roller grid in a 5-gallon bucket lets you submerge roller in paint and then squeeze out excess through mesh screen.

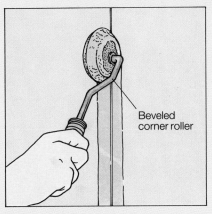

Beveled corner roller is designed to spread paint evenly in corners, avoiding paint buildup in recesses.

Slap, don't scrape, brush against side of a bucket to get a uniform, drip-free amount of paint on brush.

If you can't remove a light fixture, loosen ceiling plate and tie a plastic garbage bag around fixture to protect it.

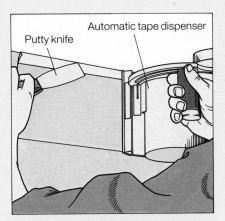

A machine that applies tape and paper at once makes masking easy. Press tape edges with a putty knife to avoid seepage.

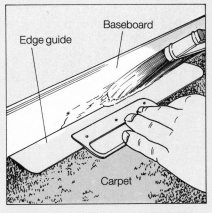

A flexible edge guide allows you to paint a baseboard below carpet line without getting paint on carpet.

The following tips from professional painters will help you do a top-quality paint job yourself.

■ For best adherence, apply all coats within about two weeks of each other.

■ Carry less paint on your brush or roller when you're working overhead than when you're painting a wall.

■ Keep a clean brush on hand for dusting trim just before painting it.

■ To remove bristles that come off your brush as you're applying paint, touch them with the tip of your wet brush; the bristles should stick to the brush. Then use a cloth to wipe the stray bristles off the brush.

■ If insects get trapped on wet paint, let it dry before brushing them off.

■ When applying an enamel finish coat, brush paint on generously and use a light touch. Avoid overbrushing when you're using enamel, since that can produce a bumpy surface. It's important to work quickly and not to try to touch up areas that you have already painted.

■ Be sure to remove masking tape before the paint dries completely so that the paint on the surface won't bond to the paint on the tape. Don't leave tape on windows in the sun or the tape will bond to the glass.

■ If you're sensitive to the smell of paint, even a paint that's relatively odorless, mix in a few drops of vanilla extract or a commercial paint fragrance additive. However, don't try to mask paint fumes—they serve as a warning to wear a respirator if you can't ventilate the area adequately.

vertical strips that go around the door panels.

Match the latch edge to the room it opens into, and the hinge edge to the room it opens away from.

For the door casing, begin with the head casing and work down the side casings. If the door opens away from the room, paint the jamb and the two surfaces of the door stop. If the door opens into the room, paint the jamb and the door side of the door stop.

Don't rehang or close the door until all the paint is thoroughly dry.

Painting cabinets

Remove any drawers and detachable shelves from the cabinets; you'll paint them separately. Before you begin to paint, clean all surfaces. Brush paint on small areas. If there are large areas to paint, you may want to use a roller.

Start painting inside the cabinet. Working from top to bottom, paint the back wall, the shelf bottoms, the side walls, and the shelf tops and edges, in that order.

Next, paint the outside from top to bottom. Then paint the inside of the doors; push them nearly closed and paint the outside. Finally, paint the drawers and shelves that you removed. Don't close the doors or return anything to the cabinet until the paint is completely dry.

CLEANING UP

Immediately after you finish using your tools, clean them. Don't delay—dry paint can make a later cleanup difficult.

Tools used with latex paint wash up easily with soap and water. Be sure to remove excess paint before washing instead of letting it go down the drain.

Use paint thinner to clean tools used with alkyd paint. Protect your hands with rubber gloves. Since you can't pour thinner down the drain or dispose of it easily, it's best to save it and reuse it. Keep the thinner in an old paint can or other container that won't be dissolved by the chemicals in the thinner. When the thinner becomes very cloudy, let the paint settle to the bottom; pour the thinner into another can. Dispose of the hard sediment.

It's not necessary to clean brushes and rollers if you plan to return to your project shortly. Brushes will keep for a few days if you hang them in the appropriate solvent; or wrap them in foil or plastic and put brushes used with alkyd paint in the freezer and those used with latex in the refrigerator. Rollers or applicators will keep overnight in a plastic bag in the refrigerator.

Cleaning brushes

Remove excess paint from brushes by brushing it out onto cardboard; or put the brush between sheets of newspaper and press down while pulling out the brush.

To clean a synthetic brush used with latex paint, hold the brush under running water until the water runs clear. Wash the brush with soap and lukewarm water, forcing water into the bristles and heel. Rinse well.

To clean a natural bristle or synthetic brush used with alkyd paint, work paint thinner into the bristles, especially at the heel, as shown below. Then use a wire brush to get out more paint. When the brush is clean, remove excess thinner by shaking the brush vigorously or lightly tapping the handle against a hard edge.

When you've finished cleaning any brush, straighten the bristles with a bristle comb. After the brush dries, wrap it in its original cover or in stiff paper. Store it flat or hang it on a nail.

Cleaning rollers & applicators

Squeeze out paint by pressing the roller or applicator against the lip of the bucket or roller tray. Scrape off caked-on paint with a putty knife. Then remove the roller cover or applicator pad.

If the cover or pad was used with latex paint, hold it under running water until the water runs clear. Wash with soap and lukewarm water, forcing water into the nap. Rinse, squeeze

---

■ CLEANING A BRUSH

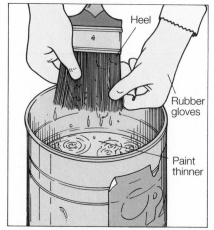

Use your gloved hands to work paint thinner into bristles of a brush used with alkyd paint.

After you've cleaned any brush, prolong its life by running a bristle comb through its bristles to straighten them.

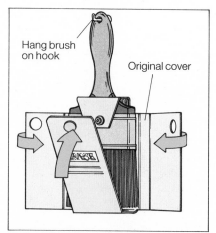

When brush is dry, wrap it in its original cover or in a piece of stiff paper. Hang brush on a wall or store flat.

out excess water, and blot lightly with a clean, absorbent cloth. Let dry completely. Wash the frame in soap and water.

To clean a cover or pad used with alkyd paint, wash it in paint thinner, forcing thinner into the nap. After it's clean, squeeze out excess thinner. (Since covers and pads are fairly inexpensive, you may prefer to dispose of those used with alkyd paint.) Wash the roller or frame in thinner.

Store clean roller covers and applicator pads in plastic bags. Place roller covers on end to allow any water or paint thinner to drain and to prevent the nap from flattening.

Cleaning yourself

Wet or dry latex paint readily washes off skin. Latex that has dried doesn't wash off clothing, however, so be sure to launder paint-encrusted clothes before the paint has dried completely.

A mechanic's hand cleaner will remove alkyd paint. It's easier on your skin than paint thinner and just as effective. Use hand cleaner, not thinner, on fresh alkyd paint on your clothing; launder the clothes immediately.

If you decide to use thinner to remove alkyd paint from your skin, rub it lightly on any spots on your hands and arms. Use a cloth dipped in thinner to dab at paint on your neck and face, being extremely careful to keep the cloth away from your eyes. Wash with soap and water and apply a lotion.

Storing paint

Most leftover paint can be stored in a tightly closed can for several months or more. If less than a quarter of the paint in a can remains, transfer it to a container small enough to be almost filled. Less air in the can means the paint is less likely to dry out.

Wipe paint from the rim of the can to permit an airtight seal and to keep paint from spattering when you replace the lid. Then firmly hammer the lid on the can.

It's best to store paint thinner and inflammable paints (check labels) in a metal cabinet. Keep all paint products out of the reach of children, and don't store such products near a flame.

Safety Precautions

Exercise caution when working with paint. Listed here are some basic safety guidelines.

■ Carefully read the labels on paint cans for warnings about possible hazards and heed all safety instructions.

■ Keep paint and paint products out of the reach of children.

■ Always work with paint products in a well-ventilated area. Open doors and windows and use exhaust fans. Excessive inhalation of fumes from paints and solvents can cause dizziness, headaches, fatigue, and nausea. Also, keep pets out of freshly painted rooms; paint fumes are especially harmful to pet birds.

■ If you can't ventilate the area well enough to get rid of fumes, wear an approved respirator, a type of mask that will filter vapors. Respirators are available at paint and hardware stores.

■ Wear a dust mask when you're sanding to keep from breathing in dust particles.

■ Wear safety goggles when using chemical strippers or caustic cleaning compounds, or when painting overhead.

■ Lay a canvas drop cloth, not a plastic one, on the floor. It will stay in place and won't be as slippery as plastic.

■ Don't use or store paint products near a flame or heat source. Avoid smoking while painting or while using thinner.

■ Many paints and solvents are particularly harmful to skin and eyes. Be especially careful when handling or applying products that contain strong solvents; again, read the labels. Wear gloves and a respirator when necessary. Also wear gloves when you're applying paint with a sponge or rag.

■ Inspect ladders for sturdiness. Make sure all four legs are resting squarely on the floor and both cross-braces are locked in place. Never stand on the top step or the utility shelf. Never lean away from a ladder; instead, get off and move it if you can't reach a spot easily.

■ For a scaffolding plank, use a sturdy 2 by 10 that's no more than 12 feet long. If you place the plank between two ladders, position the ladders so their steps are facing each other. If you run the plank between a ladder and a sawhorse, or between a ladder and a stairway step, be sure the plank is level.

■ Clean up promptly each day, and properly dispose of soiled rags. Always spread rags soaked with alkyd paint or paint thinner outdoors and let them dry all day before throwing them in the trash.

Disposing of paint

If you bought too much paint and you don't want to store it, offer it to a friend or donate it to a local theater group for painting sets. Dispose of it only as a last resort.

If you can't give the paint away, check the laws and guidelines in your community for ways to dispose of paint. Some communities have one or two days a year when they will accept paint and some other hazardous materials for disposal.

If you only have a little left over, you can get rid of any kind of paint by painting it onto cardboard and then throwing out the dried cardboard instead of disposing of the liquid. A good way to get rid of latex paint is to solidify it by filling it with cat litter; throw away the solid paint.

Wipe out any paint buckets and roller trays with newspaper; let the newspaper dry before throwing it away. Also let rags and empty paint cans dry thoroughly before putting them into the trash. Since paint- or thinner-soaked materials can catch fire, never leave them inside to dry, even overnight. Instead, spread them outdoors until they're dry.

Decorative Painting

Brushing or rolling a solid coat of paint onto a surface produces a neat, opaque finish. But take the same paint, stretch the color and consistency, and apply it in thin translucent layers with a brush, sponge, or other implement, and you've created a finish with depth and vitality.

Those painted surfaces are sometimes called faux finishes (*faux* means false in French), but technically, the term refers to a finish that simulates something real. Some decorative finishes do deceive you into thinking that you're looking at real wood, marble, or stone. But this type of painting doesn't have to mimic anything real—it can be a simple interplay of colors or some other product of your imagination.

Most decorative painting techniques use tinted washes and glazes (see facing page) to build up rich, glowing layers of color. For the applicative techniques—sponging on, ragging on, and colorwashing—you simply apply color; for the subtractive techniques—sponging off, ragging off, dragging, marbling, and wood graining—you apply color and then remove some of it so that the background color becomes visible.

For help with color and design decisions, turn to the first chapter. Note also the basic painting information in the previous section.

Choosing a technique

If you just want to give your walls added dimension and warmth, try colorwashing. To create an abstract pattern, consider sponging or ragging. If you'd like to tie together several decorative elements in a room, a floor-to-ceiling stencil copied from a design on the curtains or rug may be the answer. Marbling is an obvious choice to lend richness to your fireplace mantel and surround.

Some techniques, such as dragging and marbling, look best on a smooth surface, since they make flaws more noticeable. Sponging and ragging are the techniques most appropriate for bumpy, irregular walls, since they camouflage imperfections.

If you don't have much experience painting, try one of the easier techniques first, such as sponging on, ragging on, colorwashing, or stenciling with a precut pattern. Sponging off, ragging off, and dragging are a little more difficult. Marbling and wood graining are among the hardest techniques to master.

Tips for success

Here's some basic information you need to know before you start to paint.

Base coat. Depending on the condition of your walls and the medium you're using, you may need to apply a base coat. An eggshell finish is recommended. The water-base mediums—latex washes and acrylic glazes—adhere best to a latex or alkyd flat or eggshell base. They don't stick well to a glossier finish, even if it's deglossed.

Oil glazes will adhere to a flat or low-luster latex or alkyd base. You can even use oil glazes over a semigloss or high-gloss finish if you sand first.

Corners. You'll need a plan for handling corners to keep paint from collecting in the recesses and to avoid smearing the work you've already done.

When using a quick-drying latex wash, decorate one wall at a time after masking adjacent ones. With a slow-drying glaze, mask the edges of two opposite walls and decorate the other ones; let the surfaces dry overnight, mask the edges of the completed walls, and then do the remaining ones.

Transparent coatings. A clear coating applied to a painted surface protects the finish, makes it washable, and can give it sheen. If you want to finish with a clear coating, look for a non-yellowing, water-base one that can be applied over any finish. Be sure to choose a product that works on walls and not just on woodwork. Most of these new coatings, which are classified as water-borne liquid plastics, varnishes, or urethanes, are available in satin, semigloss, and gloss.

■ AN ARRAY OF DECORATIVE PAINTING TOOLS

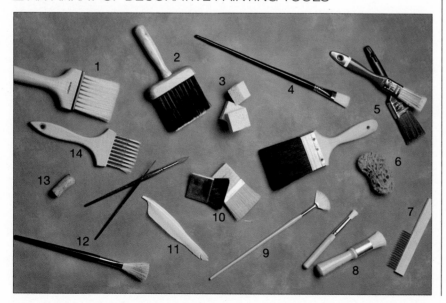

Tools for decorative painting include (1) bristle softening brush, (2) graining brush, (3) synthetic stenciling sponges, (4) artist's brush, (5) standard paintbrushes, (6) natural sea sponge, (7) comb, (8) stencil brushes, (9) fan blender, (10) mottling brushes, (11) feather, (12) artist's brushes, (13) cork, (14) pencil overgrainer.

Washes & Glazes

Most decorative painting techniques are done with washes or glazes. A wash is watered-down latex paint, and a glaze is thinned, translucent oil-base or acrylic color.

The quick-drying washes are suitable for the simpler techniques, such as sponging. The more complex techniques requiring a buildup of color, such as marbling, are best accomplished with glazes, which stay wet longer than washes and give you more time to manipulate them before they dry.

Oil or water-base?

Oil glazes, the traditional medium of decorative painters, stay wet and workable longer than either washes or acrylic glazes, and produce a wonderfully translucent finish. Mistakes are easy to correct—just dab on paint thinner and wipe off the paint. Note, however, that handling oil-base paints and paint thinner requires care because of the chemicals and fumes involved.

Acrylic glazes and latex washes are easy to use—they're mixed and cleaned up with water. Although water-base finishes generally don't last as long as oil-base ones, you can always apply a clear coating to protect the finish.

Making washes & glazes

It's not difficult to mix your own wash or glaze. Simply follow the instructions and recipes on this page.

Washes are extremely simple to make—you just mix ordinary latex paint from a paint store with water.

To make a glaze, it's easiest to start with a transparent commercial glaze—basically paint without any pigment (sources for commercial glazes are listed at right). Then add paint from a paint store—alkyd for an oil glaze, acrylic for an acrylic glaze. The intensity of the color will be thinned by the commercial glaze, producing translucent paint.

You can also use paint from an art supply store or crafts shop, but you'll need some expertise in choosing colors. Japan colors or artist's oils are compatible with oil glazes, artist's acrylics with acrylic glazes or latex washes. Use universal tints to color any medium.

To the colored glaze, add the appropriate solvent—paint thinner for an oil glaze and water for an acrylic glaze. The solvent dilutes the paint so that it can be applied in very thin coats. To extend the drying time slightly, you can add a retarding agent to an acrylic glaze.

The following recipes are just a starting point. Decorative painting isn't an exact science. In fact, it's more akin to cooking than to chemistry. Don't be afraid to experiment as you become more practiced and confident.

Latex Wash

You can vary the recipe so that water makes up from 10 to 90 percent of the mixture. The more paint you use, the more durable the finish.

1 part latex paint
2 parts water

Oil Glaze

A good general recipe for beginners, this glaze stays wet even if you work slowly. For faster drying and a harder finish, use less commercial oil glaze and more paint thinner.

1 part commercial oil glaze
1 part alkyd paint
1 part paint thinner

Acrylic Glaze #1

This glaze recipe is suitable for ragging, sponging, and simple marbling. Change the proportions to 5 parts commercial acrylic glaze, 1 part paint, and 1 part water for decorative techniques requiring greater translucency, such as dragging, wood graining, and more sophisticated marbling.

1 part commercial acrylic glaze
2 parts acrylic paint
1 part water
2–4 oz. retarder per gallon (optional)

Acrylic Glaze #2

Use this recipe if you don't have easy access to a commercial acrylic glaze. Look for acrylic gel medium in an art supply store.

1 part acrylic gel medium
1 part acrylic paint
2 parts water
2–4 oz. retarder per gallon (optional)

Finding commercial glazes

Listed below are sources for transparent commercial glazes.

Sources for oil glazes

Liberty Paint Corp.
969 Columbia Street
Hudson, NY 12534
(518) 828-4060

McCloskey Co.
7600 State Road
Philadelphia, PA 19136
(800) 345-4530

Benjamin Moore & Co.
Pratt & Lambert, Inc.
(See Yellow Pages under "Paint")

Sources for acrylic glazes

Cal-Western Paints Inc.
11748 Slauson Avenue
Santa Fe Springs, CA 90670
(213) 723-6362

Janovic Plaza
1150 Third Avenue
New York, NY 10021
(212) 772-1400

Liberty Paint Corp.
969 Columbia Street
Hudson, NY 12534
(518) 828-4060

The easiest technique for a beginner, sponging involves using a natural sea sponge to make mottled impressions on a surface. Either you can "sponge on" (sponge one or more colors onto the surface), or you can "sponge off" (use the sponge to remove wet paint).

Sponging off generally produces a more subtle effect than sponging on. For both applications, you can use a latex wash or a glaze. If you decide to use a latex wash for sponging off, thin the paint only slightly instead of making the standard wash.

The look that you'll achieve depends on the colors you select. A pastel color over on off-white background will produce a fresh, cheery effect; a dark color over a light background will create a bold, dramatic look; and variations of the same color will give the surface a feeling of depth. When you use more than one color to sponge on, the color you apply last will be the most dominant one.

The effect also depends on the type of sponge you choose and the way in which you wield it. A large, flat sea sponge is best for this technique. If you have a round sea sponge, cut it in half to get a flat surface. Medium-size pores are preferred—small pores produce a fussy pattern, and large pores create a coarse look. The sponge imprints look most effective when they're applied with uniform pressure randomly over the surface. Be sure to keep changing the position of the sponge as you work.

Look for sea sponges in home decorating and art stores, in bath shops, and in cosmetic departments of drugstores and health food stores. Ask for a wool sponge rather than a grass one.

Sponging is suitable for walls, ceilings, doors, and even furniture, though not intricately carved pieces. The surface doesn't have to be perfectly smooth, since sponging hides flaws.

SPONGING ON

1 After moistening sponge in water and wringing it well, dip it into first wash or glaze and squeeze until it just barely stops dripping.

2 Dab surface lightly with sponge, rotating it when you lift it to vary pattern you're creating. Reload sponge periodically when color begins to fade.

3 Dab sponge into corners as well as you can; be careful not to jam it in, or color will be heavier there than elsewhere.

4 In corner areas where sponge will not reach, use a fine artist's brush to make dots simulating mottled impressions of sponge.

5 Let entire sponged surface dry completely. If desired, apply a second color, following same procedure.

6 Let second sponged color dry completely. If desired, apply a third color. Final result should be a pleasing blend of colors.

1 Begin by cutting in at a corner, brushing on wash or glaze solidly in only a small area (no more than 15 inches long).

2 Moisten a clean sponge in water and wring it well. Before wash or glaze dries, dab surface with sponge, using a blotting motion.

3 Continue applying wash or glaze to a small area at a time (no more than 3 square feet); dab wet surface with sponge, changing its position as you work to vary pattern. When sponge becomes saturated with wash or glaze, rinse in appropriate solvent; then wash in soapy water and squeeze dry.

DRAGGING

Dragging consists of creating thin stripes on a surface. First you apply a glaze or wash to the surface (a glaze is easier for beginners); then you "drag" downward with a brush or other tool to reveal narrow stripes of the background color. Or use the alternate one-step method shown below, at right.

The pattern can be neat and uniform or rough and irregular, depending on the dragging tool you use. Dragging with a brush is traditional; you can buy special dragging brushes, but an inexpensive paintbrush will do just as well. Or you can use cheesecloth, a comb sold for decorative painting, or a device you make yourself, such as a squeegee in which you've cut notches.

Dragging can be used by itself or in wood graining (see page 58). Walls, doors, and furniture are good candidates for dragging. Just be sure the surface is smooth and regular—dragging emphasizes imperfections.

The technique requires speed to drag a section before it dries, as well as some care to keep stripes parallel. You may want a helper—one person can apply the glaze or wash while the other immediately applies the dragging tool.

1 Brush on glaze or wash from top to bottom and from side to side, covering only a narrow strip at a time (no more than 18 inches wide) so area is still wet while you drag.

2 Position a large, dry paintbrush at top of strip and press hard so that bristles bend back to heel of brush. Drag brush down length of surface. Wipe brush on a rag after each pass.

Alternative method. Instead of brushing on glaze or wash, dip wadded cheesecloth into glaze or wash and drag it downward in narrow strips.

A relatively easy technique for a beginner, ragging consists of pressing a soft cotton rag onto a wet surface to make a textured impression.

You can "rag on" (apply one or more colors to the surface with a rag), or you can "rag off" (use the rag to remove wet paint). The two techniques are shown below and on the facing page. A latex wash or a glaze is suitable for either technique, though it's much easier to rag off a glaze since it stays wet longer than a wash. A latex wash is ideal for ragging on.

The effect you achieve depends both on the type of rag or other material you choose and how you maneuver it. A soft cotton cloth works best because it absorbs the glaze or wash, is easy to manipulate, and doesn't show hard edges when it's pressed against the surface. Old cotton napkins and new T-shirts are good choices. Avoid using old T-shirts—the fabric has been stretched out too much to leave a good impression.

Just be sure the cloths you choose are clean and lint free, and plan to use the same material throughout the procedure. Cut the cloths into 1½- or 2-foot squares, making sure there are no frayed edges.

It's easy to vary the effect of ragging. Simply change the pressure you're using on the rag, roll it around on the surface, or rearrange its shape occasionally as you're working.

The effect also depends on your colors. To create a dramatic effect, select bold, contrasting colors, such as red on a yellow background; for a more subtle look, use soft or pastel colors; to achieve a sense of depth, try variations of the same color. No matter how many colors you use, always let some of the background show through.

Ragging is suitable for walls, ceilings, doors, and furniture.

RAGGING ON

1 Immerse a clean, dry, lint-free rag in first wash or glaze and wring out well.

2 Loosely bunch up rag and lightly press on surface. To vary pattern, rebunch and rotate rag as you work. When color begins to fade, reload rag.

3 Press rag into corners as well as you can; be careful not to jam it in, or color will be heavier there than elsewhere.

4 In corner areas where rag will not reach, use an artist's brush to simulate ragging pattern.

5 Let entire ragged surface dry completely. If desired, apply a second color, following same procedure.

6 Let second ragged color dry completely. Apply a third color, if desired. Final finish should be an attractive blend of colors.

RAGGING OFF

1 Begin by cutting in at a corner, brushing on wash or glaze solidly in only a small area (no more than 15 inches long).

2 Press a clean, dry, bunched-up rag as far into corner as possible; don't be concerned if color is a little darker in corners than on flat surfaces.

3 Continue applying wash or glaze to a small area at a time (no more than 6 square feet). Blot wet surface with a dry, bunched-up rag; to vary pattern, rebunch and rotate rag as you work. When rag becomes saturated with wash or glaze, switch to a clean one.

Other Ways to Make an Impression

Rags and sponges aren't the only materials you can use to make interesting, intriguing patterns on walls, furniture, and other surfaces. You can press into service any number of items found around the home, such as wax paper, plastic wrap, paper bags, burlap, a feather duster, or a small squeegee into which you have cut notches.

A feather purchased from an art store is another "tool" that you can use to make a pleasing pattern. Each object leaves its own unique imprint when it's used to apply, push around, or lift off paint. (Impressions left by some easily found materials are illustrated below.) Just make sure that whatever you use is clean and lint free.

Regardless of the material you choose, you'll find that it's easier to make impressions in a glaze rather than in a wash, since a glaze stays wet longer than a wash. If you're working with a nonabsorbent material, such as plastic wrap or wax paper, you'll need a plentiful supply since glaze will build up rapidly on it.

■ WAX PAPER

■ PLASTIC WRAP

■ PAPER BAG

■ FEATHER

COLORWASHING

One of the simplest techniques for painting walls, colorwashing consists of building up very thin layers of translucent color for a rich, warm glow. A colorwashed surface lends itself to country and other informal types of decor.

Below are instructions for colorwashing with a glaze and three different methods for colorwashing with latex washes or undiluted latex paint. Glazes produce a richer, more dramatic finish than either latex washes or undiluted latex paint; they're also much easier to work with than the other choices because they stay wet longer.

Generally, the thinner the coat you apply, the richer the result. You can use variations of the same color or different but related colors. A lighter-colored glaze applied over a darker one will give you a chalky, aged effect. A darker glaze over a lighter one will produce a wonderful translucent quality.

The effect you achieve will also depend on the tool you use—brush, rag, cheesecloth, or sponge—and how you manipulate it.

Colorwashing is suitable for walls, ceilings, and furniture. It also makes an attractive background when you're stenciling. Since the technique emphasizes any imperfections on the surface, it's a particularly good choice for rough, flawed walls when you're looking for a rustic appearance.

COLORWASHING WITH A GLAZE

1 Brush on a thin layer of first glaze (solvent should make up from 70 to 90 percent of glaze) in small, irregular patches. For best results, vary size and shape of patches.

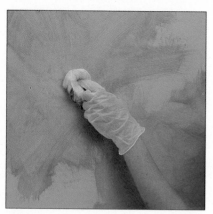

2 While glaze is still wet, blend out with a clean, dry cotton rag or a piece of cheesecloth; or use a large, dry paintbrush. Wipe off glaze until you achieve desired effect.

3 When surface is thoroughly dry, apply second glaze in a thin layer, following same procedure as for first glaze. Apply as many glazes as desired.

COLORWASHING WITH WASHES OR UNDILUTED LATEX PAINT

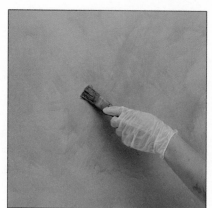

Method 1. Brush on three or four successive layers of very thin washes (9 parts water to 1 part paint), allowing each wash to dry thoroughly before applying next one. Don't paint carefully, but rather slap on each wash quickly and haphazardly.

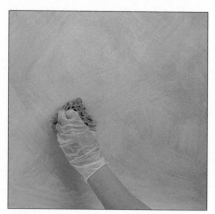

Method 2. Brush on a thin wash (4 parts water to 1 part paint) in small, irregular patches (cover no more than 6 square feet at a time); then blur wet brush marks with a clean, damp sponge or paintbrush.

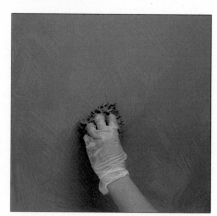

Method 3. On background of same color value as paint you're applying, use a natural sea sponge to smear on and push around undiluted latex paint in irregular patches.

54 *Paint*

Painting Furniture

Sponging, marbling, stenciling, and other decorative painting techniques are easy, inexpensive, and fun ways to liven up tables, chairs, bookcases, and other furniture. Such techniques give new life to run-down or worn-out pieces, beautifully disguise ugly pieces, and smarten up products made of inferior wood. Painted furniture lends individuality to your decor and adds color and texture where they're least expected.

Painting furniture is an ideal project for novice painters. It's a lot easier to start with a small piece of furniture, such as a coffee table or low chest, than to tackle a wall. Consider buying an end table or other small item at a junk shop or garage sale for practice.

The prospect of painting furniture becomes even more attractive when you realize that you don't have to strip the piece before you paint it. Although getting down to bare wood or metal is ideal, don't bother if it looks like too much work. Just clean the surface and sand it smooth.

No matter what material you're using, you'll most likely have to prime before painting. The type of primer required depends on the existing surface (see page 33 or ask your paint dealer).

Any of the techniques discussed on pages 50–60 are suitable for furniture. You may also want to try two other techniques—spattering and stippling—commonly used on furniture. Both are illustrated below.

Spattering. This technique consists of showering the surface with flecks of paint. To cause the shower, you simply hit the handle of a loaded paintbrush against the handle of a dry brush or stick held perpendicular to your paintbrush; or flick the bristles of the loaded brush with your fingers. For small, fine flecks, dilute the paint, but not so much that it runs.

Stippling. This technique involves reorganizing a wet glaze into a mass of dots. Since the finish is subtle, bold colors are best for the glaze and background.

After brushing on the glaze, you dab the surface with the tip of a brush. Specialized stippling brushes are expensive, but you can use an ordinary stiff-bristled paintbrush, a stainer's brush, a scrub brush, or even a toothbrush.

■ SPATTERING

■ STIPPLING

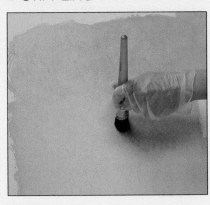

Spattering this small wood toy chest with vivid shades of red, blue, green, and purple has given it individuality and appeal. Paintbrush in front of chest is faux—it was painted on floor cloth. Decorative painting: Ann Blair Davison.

MARBLING WITH A GLAZE

Marbling with a glaze, the traditional method for marbling, requires a lot of practice and a good sense of timing—the surface can't be too wet or too dry when you work it. (For instructions on how to marble with latex washes, see the facing page.)

The technique consists of applying a tinted glaze over a nonporous background, building fields of color, and creating a network of veins over the surface. You then soften and blur the design before applying the final veins. (Plan to complete an entire small area before starting on a new one.) Finally, the thoroughly dry surface is covered with a transparent coating to give it a uniform sheen and to protect the finished design.

With this technique you can simulate real marble or create your own design. You may not want to marble all the walls in a room—the job can be overwhelming and very difficult to accomplish. But a well-positioned marble panel in the middle of one wall may be just the right touch. Dividing the space into rectangles and completing each one in turn makes the work easier.

Marbling is also suitable for fireplace surrounds, moldings, doors, and furniture. Don't try to marble ornately carved woodwork if you're a beginner.

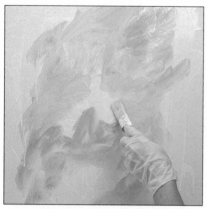

1 On a small area (no more than 6 square feet), brush on a background glaze to match color of surface you're marbling.

2 Using additional glazes in other colors, paint irregular shapes, or drifts, over wet surface. After applying each glaze, rag it off (blot with a dry, bunched-up rag, rebunching and rotating rag as you work to vary pattern). Expect some blending of colors.

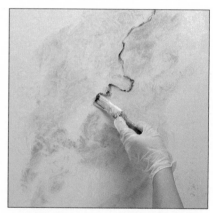

3 Put a dab of paint (artist's oils for oil glaze, artist's acrylics for acrylic glaze) on one side of brush tip; holding side of brush without paint against surface, make veins, using a light, shaky motion. (Paint from other side of brush will come through.) Blot veins with a dry rag.

4 Wait several seconds for glaze to dry slightly; then soften and blur it lightly with a blending brush held at a right angle to surface or with crumpled tissue paper. If you blend when glaze is too wet, you'll smear or streak it.

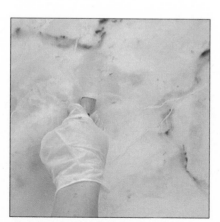

5 Make additional veins by scraping through glaze with edge of a cork, using a shaky, squiggly motion. Blot veins with a dry rag or crumpled tissue paper, or soften them with blending brush.

6 Apply a small amount of thinned paint (use a color that will stand out from others) to a fine liner brush or to tip of a feather. While supporting your elbow with your free hand, make final veins with a light, shaky touch. Continue to next small area, following same procedure.

MARBLING WITH LATEX WASHES

Although marbling with a glaze is the traditional method, it's also possible to create an interesting marbled surface using latex washes.

Working on a surface with a solid-color background (an existing painted surface is fine, provided it's smooth and in good condition), you build up subtle layers of color and veining. Each layer that you apply blurs and softens the previous layers. The result is a finished surface with an unexpected feeling of depth and dimension.

The advantage of using latex washes is that the procedure doesn't require the same sense of timing needed for marbling with a glaze, since each wash layer dries quickly. When you're finished applying the washes and making the veins, cover the surface with a transparent coating to protect it and give it a sheen.

With this technique, you can copy a specific type of marble, if you wish, or create your own impression of marble. Marbling entire walls and other large surfaces is much easier to accomplish with latex washes than it is with a glaze.

Marbling with latex washes is also an appropriate decorative technique for moldings, fireplace surrounds, doors, and furniture.

1 Use a natural sea sponge to dab on first latex wash in irregular shapes, or drifts. As wash is applied, blot wet surface with a clean, damp sponge to spread drifts and soften them. Work over entire area, applying wash in drifts and blotting to spread them as you go.

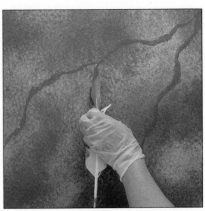

2 With a light, shaky touch, make veins over entire surface, using a feather dipped into thinned latex paint or artist's acrylics. (Use same color as background to create look of fissures.)

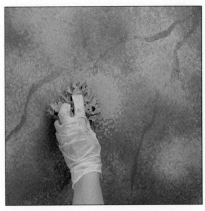

3 Using another color, sponge on a second wash in drifts, blotting each drift before it dries. Cover some areas not coated by first wash, and sponge over first wash in other areas.

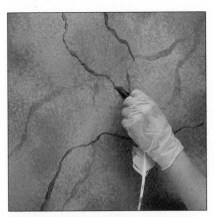

4 Make additional veins in another color, as described in Step 2.

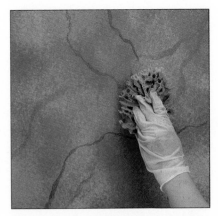

5 Using a third color, sponge on another wash in drifts, blotting as you go. (Using same color as background for third wash will give you increased depth.) Cover some areas not touched when you did first and second washes, and sponge over portions of previous washes.

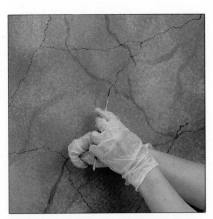

6 Using a color that will stand out from others, make final veins over entire surface with a fine liner brush or tip of a feather; use a light, shaky touch while supporting your working hand with your free hand.

Creating a fantasy grain, one that approximates a real wood grain or that is simply a product of your imagination, is among the most difficult finishes to do well. Still, it doesn't require as much practice or expertise as authentic wood graining and can lend almost the same appeal.

Applying a dark brown glaze over a background of canary yellow will give the wood finish a realistic look, but you can just as easily use reds, blues, or other colors that strike your fancy. Similar colors work well together; apply the darker shade over the lighter one. To create the graining pattern, use a pencil overgrainer or other instrument, such as a cork. Once the finish is dry, apply a transparent coating to the surface to protect it and give it luster.

Below are instructions for two different types of wood graining. For the first, you drag the surface with a paintbrush or with cheesecloth; or, as an alternative method, you can flog it. Then you choose from a variety of brushes or other tools to give the surface the effect you want. For the second type, a mottled grain, you swirl the glaze with a mottling brush.

Fantasy wood graining is suitable for wall panels, doors, moldings, cabinets, and furniture.

SIMPLE WOOD GRAINING

1 After applying glaze to a panel or other small area (if you're a beginner, cover no more than 6 square feet at a time), drag wet surface with an ordinary paintbrush or with cheesecloth. (For instructions on dragging, see page 51.) Dragged surface can be completed grain, or you can proceed to Step 2.

Alternative method. After applying glaze, flog wet surface (pat with flat of a brush using a quick, bouncing motion, always going away from yourself). Flogged surface can be completed grain, or you can proceed to Step 2.

2 On either a dragged or flogged surface, create wood grain, using a pencil overgrainer (shown here), an artist's brush, a fan overgrainer, or a homemade tool, such as stiff cardboard or a small squeegee carved with notches.

MOTTLED GRAIN

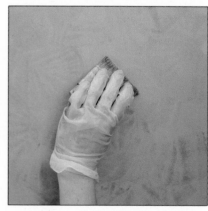

1 With a paintbrush, apply glaze to a panel or other small area, using a scumbling, or sideways scratching, motion. (If you're a beginner, cover no more than 6 square feet at a time.)

2 Holding mottling brush in palm of your hand, press your fingertips into bristles.

3 Using mottling brush as shown at left, push wet glaze around in curves or other swirling shapes. For best results, keep pattern irregular.

Although truly realistic wood graining is an art requiring years of practice, you may want to try it. Even if the finish you create doesn't fool a botanist, it can still be very pleasing.

Wood grainers have traditionally chosen expensive, exotic woods, such as mahogany, to copy. Mahogany has two main types of grain: arched heartwood and straight graining. You can simulate both with a brush called a fan overgrainer. For a special treatment, create a central panel framed by rails (horizontal pieces) and stiles (vertical pieces). The finished surface will be neater if you mask off one area from the other when painting the design.

Ask the paint store to mix a color that duplicates the rich, warm hue of mahogany. Or do it yourself, mixing equal parts of burnt sienna, alizarin crimson, and raw umber, using artist's oils in an oil glaze or artist's acrylics in an acrylic glaze. Some professionals paint over a dirty pink base coat; others like a reddish yellow background. Finish with a glossy clear coating.

Mahogany graining is suitable for wall panels, doors, moldings, cabinets, and furniture.

1 After brushing glaze on a panel or other surface, flog wet surface (pat with flat of a brush using a quick, bouncing motion, always going away from yourself).

2 To simulate mahogany heartwood, make a series of arches, using a fan overgrainer. Dip brush into paint, dabbing off excess; then spread bristles with fingertips. Hold brush nearly parallel to surface and at a right angle to arches you're creating.

3 Soften grains with a bristle softening brush held at a right angle to surface.

4 With fan overgrainer, make a straight grain at a slight angle on one side of arched heartwood; repeat on other side.

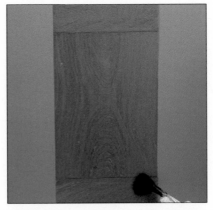

5 If your design calls for rails, brush glaze above and below completed central panel; then flog at a slight angle away from panel. Use fan overgrainer to make horizontal arches—those on rail above panel should go in opposite direction from those on rail below panel. Brush lightly with softening brush.

6 Brush glaze on side pieces, or stiles, brushing up to completed central panel; then flog at a slight angle away from panel. Use fan overgrainer to make straight grains at a slight angle away from central panel. Brush lightly with softening brush.

STENCILING

One of the simplest and most inexpensive ways to decorate a surface, stenciling allows you to express your individuality in a colorful and lively way.

Stenciling doesn't have to be limited to borders at the tops of walls. You can use it on a door, over an entire wall or ceiling, on a fireplace surround, or around a window frame. A stencil is most often repeated, but a single stenciled design on a cabinet door or wall panel can be just the right touch.

You can choose a precut stencil, or you can make your own (instructions appear on the facing page). Your design can call for a single color or two or more colors. It's best to stencil over a flat, eggshell, or satin finish—the paint you use for stenciling won't adhere well to a glossier surface.

You can use ordinary latex paint for stenciling, or you can choose paint from an art store. Among artist's paints, the easiest to use are artist's acrylics, which are water soluble and provide intense, quick-drying color. Although japan colors dry instantly, they're flat and require paint thinner for mixing and cleanup. Artist's oils, also soluble in paint thinner, are extremely difficult to use for stenciling, since they dry very slowly and smudge easily.

Regardless of the paint you use, mix it to a thick, pasty (not runny) consistency.

Measure the width (or height, for vertical placement) of the surface to determine how many stencil repeats will fit. Arrange the designs from the center of the surface out to the edges so corners will match. You may want to reduce the space between designs so they'll be complete at the corners.

To apply the paint, use either a small-celled synthetic sponge or a short, blunt-bristled stencil brush; you may find the sponge easier to manipulate than the brush.

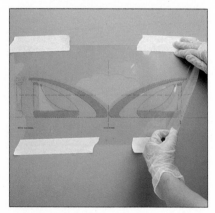

1 Measure and mark stencil placement guidelines with a steel tape measure and pencil or a chalk line. Secure first stencil to surface with masking tape. (Use type of tape that won't mar painted surfaces.)

2 Dip sponge or stencil brush into paint; then tap on scrap paper or a paper plate to get rid of excess paint. (Too much paint on sponge or brush allows paint to seep under edges of stencil.)

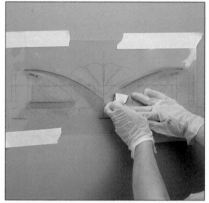

3 Apply paint by pouncing sponge or brush (tapping it directly against surface) or by using it in a circular motion; work from outside of each shape toward center.

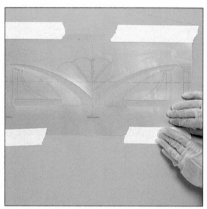

4 After all shapes are filled in, carefully remove first stencil; then tape second stencil to surface, aligning designs.

5 Apply paint to second and any subsequent stencils, following same procedure.

6 After completed stenciled design is dry, touch up any smudges with paint used for background finish.

Making Your Own Stencil

Although a wide selection of precut stencils is available today, you may want to make your own, perhaps so you can match a decorative element already present in the room or so you can carry out a particular theme. Fortunately, you don't have to be an artist for this job, since it isn't necessary to create the design yourself. You can copy a design that you like or trace one from a book of stencils. If the prototype isn't the right size, simply enlarge or reduce it on a copying machine.

The number of stencils required depends on how many colors you're using and how intricate the design is. Each color should be on a separate stencil, unless the sections that are to be painted in different colors are spaced far apart. You'll also need separate stencils if the design has many small pieces or lines running close together, even if they're the same color.

Gathering supplies

Clear acetate (.0075 gauge) is the easiest material to use for stencils since it's transparent and allows you to layer as many sheets as you need and still see the original design clearly. You can layer up to four sheets of frosted mylar (.005 gauge), but you won't be able to see through them as easily. Stencil board is opaque and doesn't allow you to see additional stencils underneath.

You'll need colored pencils or markers, a utility or craft knife, a supply of sharp blades, a ruler, masking tape, and a good cutting surface.

To transfer the design onto the stencil material, use a technical drawing pen and India ink. A black felt-tip pen also works on mylar. However, transferring the design may not be necessary if you use a photocopy as a guide for cutting the stencil (see at right).

Transferring the design

Draw the design to the desired size on graph paper. If you're copying from a stencil book, the design will already have bridges, narrow strips that link the parts of the design and keep the stencil from falling apart. Otherwise, you must put in bridges yourself by breaking the design into logical segments and placing bridges there. Color the completed design with appropriately colored pencils or markers so that you'll know which shapes to cut on each stencil.

Trim the stencil material to the size of the design, leaving a 1-inch margin on all sides. Tape the first piece of stencil material over the design and trace the areas that will be painted in the first color. If you're using more than one stencil, leave the first one in place and tape additional ones on top.

To make registration marks on each stencil, use a dotted line to trace a section of the design. Don't cut on this line; use it for aligning the new stencil with the pattern.

Mark the top front side of each stencil, and number the stencils in their order of application.

Cutting the stencils

Place the stencils, one at a time, on a flat, firm cutting surface. Using a utility or craft knife, cut the stencil, drawing the knife toward you in a smooth, continuous movement. When you're cutting curves, turn the design rather than the knife. Trim any jagged edges. Don't worry if the cut edges aren't perfect: any slight flaws won't be noticeable in the finished work.

Using photocopies

If you have a clear photocopy of the design in the exact size needed, you don't have to draw the design on the stencil material. (Note, however, that you will have to draw in bridges if there aren't any in the design.) You can simply attach the photocopy to the stencil material and use it as a cutting guide. You'll need a separate photocopy for each color in the design; use colored pencils or markers to fill in the color.

To cut from a photocopied design, coat the back of each photocopy with spray adhesive and press it on the stencil material. To make sure it's securely attached, tape the edges of the photocopy to the stencil.

On each stencil cut all the areas that will be painted the same color. Then cut registration marks on each sheet so the stencils will align. After each stencil is cut, remove the photocopy.

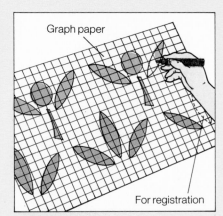

Transfer design to graph paper, being careful to include bridges between elements so stencil won't fall apart. Using pencils or markers, color design appropriately.

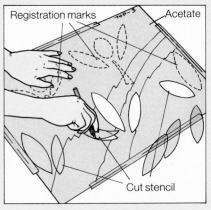

Use a separate sheet for each color in design, unless elements are spaced far apart. Label sheets and add registration marks. Then cut stencils.

Wallpaper

A WORLD OF CHOICES

It's hard to beat wallpaper for versatility. Wallpaper can go in just about any room of the house—kitchen, family room, bathroom, living room, dining room, and bedroom. Depending on its color and pattern, wallpaper can play a starring role in the room, setting the decorating style, mood, and tone, or it can simply stand in as a soft, subtle background for furnishings. Moreover, wallpaper is available in a myriad of colors, styles, textures, and patterns, as well as in a variety of materials, from scrubbable vinyl to delicate hand-screened paper.   Glance through the colorful examples presented on the following pages. Whether your preference is for traditional florals and stripes with old-world charm or sleek, contemporary designs that mimic marble or granite, you're sure to find a number of appealing treatments.   But finding the right design is only one step in a successful wallpapering project. Equally important is choosing the appropriate wall-covering material, preparing the walls so they're clean and smooth, and, finally, hanging the paper correctly. Whether you're a novice at wallpapering or you have some experience, the information in this chapter can guide you every step of the way.

A unified look is a real eye-pleaser. Here, coordinated wallpapers, border paper, and fabric combine for a sophisticated yet relaxed feeling. The floral pattern sets the room's tone; the background stripes are repeated in the paper below the border and in the fabric on the window and furniture. Interior design: Michelle Raimondi of Raimondi's Paint & Wallpaper and Stephen M. Boyce.

BOLDLY PATTERNED TO CLASSICALLY SIMPLE

Making a strong statement, this striking wallpaper with sofa upholstered in a matching fabric works well because the other design elements—wood flooring, subtly patterned chairs, and glass-topped table—are more mild-mannered. Design: Pierre Deux Original Fabrics.

The perfect background for a collection of majolica plates, this lattice-style wallpaper complements the room's European country flavor without calling attention to itself. Interior design: Barbara McDowell.

Create visual interest in a small space with a very dramatic paper. Although the style of this wall covering evokes antiquity, the metallic surface is clearly contemporary. Interior design: Hendrix/Alardyce.

CREATING AN ILLUSION

The trompe l'oeil design of this "library" wallpaper makes a tiny space seem larger—and more interesting. The paper's rich, traditional colors and feeling are echoed in the medieval tapestry-style throw pillows. The "wood" border just behind the sofa reinforces the design's realism. Interior design: Catherine Campbell Interiors.

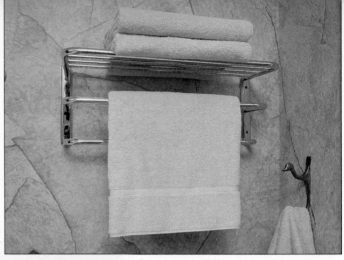

Custom-torn paper applied in overlapping layers on the bathroom walls simulates the look of marble without the expense. Create your own custom-designed wallpaper from other "found" materials, such as art prints, doilies, blueprints, children's drawings, photographs, even plain brown paper. Interior design: Carlene Anderson of Kitchen Design Inc.

Although this wall surface resembles the painting technique known as dragging, it's actually wallpaper. The subtle striping provides a supportive but not distracting background for artwork, molding details, and furnishings. Interior design: Mona Branagh of Pacific Bay Interiors.

BOLD, BEAUTIFUL BORDERS

Borders galore define and outline the walls and ceiling in this cheery bedroom. Because it's nondirectional, the floral border can run vertically and horizontally—on the ceiling, below the ceiling molding, above and below the chair rail, just above the baseboards, around the window, and down the walls at the corners. The striped wallpaper lets the border and its coordinated fabric occupy center stage. Interior design: Kelly Heim.

Custom border designs like the one shown here require careful planning and attention to detail. The gold rococo border features square cutouts at the corners; the elevation change allows the floral cutout to blossom onto the wall. Interior design: Sandra Keating of Nesting Instincts.

A border with a message allows a child to lay claim to his or her special place in this shared bedroom. Repeating the border above the window helps to unify the separate spaces. Interior design: Chet Setterlund.

PERSONAL EXPRESSIONS

Because the images and colors on the walls of this bathroom reflect the style and ambience of the room, the result is harmonious and pleasing, even though there's a lot going on. Interior design: Lequita Vance-Watkins.

Traditional and crisp, the striped wallpaper in this bedroom sets the stage for a full range of decorative elements. The stenciled floral-and-bow pattern takes its colors and motifs from the wallpaper and from the coordinated fabric on the window, bed, and chair. Interior design: Jeanese Rowell Interiors. Decorative painting: Karen Sickel.

A fantasy world of larger-than-life images splashes across the walls of this bathroom. Actually painted canvas hung in strips, the wall covering was designed with open background color in the corners to make it easier to join the strips. The wall-mounted fixture was painted to continue the design. Decorative painting: The Beardsley Company.

Capturing the best of the past, the reproduction wallpapers in this Victorian room are richly ornamented with geometric figures, swirls, and fancy shapes. Multiple adjoining borders and ornate detail on every surface are characteristic of the era. Design: Bradbury & Bradbury Art Wallpapers.

Choosing Wallpaper

The "right" wallpaper not only appeals to you but also works well in your setting. Wallpaper can set or support a color scheme; it can emphasize or "alter" the room's size or shape; it can also serve as the room's focal point.

With the seemingly endless number of sample books in most wallpaper stores, you may wonder how you'll ever find just the right wallpaper. The best strategy is to have a clear idea of what your wallpaper should look like, where you'll hang it, and what material it should be. Then you can start thumbing through wallpaper books. After several sessions, you'll be able to narrow your choices and decide on the one that's perfect for you.

TAKING STOCK

The best place to begin is with your own surroundings. Notice the different wallpapers you see in the homes of friends, in restaurants, in decorators' showhouses, and in magazines. Examine the photos on pages 62–72. Then take a long, careful look around you— your house and furnishings play a major role in determining the kind of wallpaper you'll want to consider.

When you're ready to shop, bring along samples of upholstery fabric, carpet, and other colors you plan to use; a photograph of the room with its furnishings may help you visualize how different wallpapers will look. Also have with you a diagram of the room with its dimensions clearly marked.

It's best to have some idea of the "look" you're trying to achieve. Here are some design pointers. For details on general color and design principles, see pages 5–15.

Style. Whether your home is contemporary or traditional, Early American or Southwestern, or something quite different, your wallpaper can reflect the style that gives your home its character. Or, you may want to use wallpaper to develop a special feeling or style for a particular room.

Manufacturers often sort wallpaper into books by style. If you're not sure of what you want, looking through a variety of wallpaper books can help you put a name to your ideas.

Color. Try to decide on one or more colors you would like to see on the walls; perhaps you can even determine which color should dominate and which colors you'll use as highlights. And don't ignore solid-color papers—a single-color textile, for example, can soften a large expanse of wall.

Decide what background color— white, cream, ivory, or perhaps something darker—works for you. A light background color helps brighten a dark room; a darker color makes a room appear smaller but adds drama, even in a small space. If the room you're papering is bright and sunny, avoid shiny finishes; they'll just create glare.

Scale and pattern. The size and pattern of the design elements in the wallpaper will affect the appearance of the room. Make sure you understand these aspects of design, discussed in the first chapter, before you choose your wallpaper.

Where to wallpaper

Do you want to paper the whole room or just one wall? Does a chair rail or other decorative molding suggest the use of two papers rather than one? Would a border along the ceiling line work well?

Installed on just one wall, wallpaper lends color to the room and foreshortens it. You can even combine multiple wall coverings on a single wall if you use a chair rail or a border in between; if so, hang the darker, heavier pattern on the bottom.

Borders are an easy—and relatively inexpensive—way to lend elegance and charm to a room. You can combine a border with wallpaper or use it alone on a painted wall. Borders look great at the ceiling line just below a crown molding; where there's no molding, a border compensates for its lack. A border at chair-rail height often lends a traditional feeling to a room. (In tight quarters, however, a chair rail makes a room seem smaller.)

If you have artwork on your walls, consider hanging a textile wall covering or a subtly striped one that won't detract from your art.

Choices in materials

Often, the use the room receives will suggest the best material for the wall covering. For example, although most children's areas need only washable paper, a scrubbable one will stand up better to rough treatment and thorough cleaning. The material content of a wall covering is a determining factor not only in its durability and cleanability, but also in its appearance, cost, installation, and ease of removal.

The back of a wallpaper sample usually contains information on the wallpaper's content, whether it's washable or scrubbable, and whether it can be stripped or peeled from the wall. You can also check there to learn the size of its pattern repeat.

Vinyls. The most popular wallpapers, especially for do-it-yourselfers, have some vinyl content. Vinyl's durability and strength make these papers relatively easy to install; they're also easy to maintain.

■ *Fabric-backed vinyl.* This type of wallpaper has a vinyl top layer and an undersurface of fiberglass or cheesecloth. The sturdiest kind of wallpaper, fabric-backed vinyl is washable, often scrubbable, and usually strippable. Compared with other papers, it's also more moisture resistant and less likely to tear if a wall cracks. Fabric-backed vinyl usually comes unpasted because it's often too heavy to roll well if prepasted.

Fiberglass-backed wallpapers often have a smooth surface. Those with cheesecloth backing may be thicker and have some texture, which tends to hide surface imperfections.

Hand-done silk screening produces a wall covering characterized by rich colors and distinctive artistry. Selvage edges of such hand-screened papers require trimming before paper can be hung.

■ *Paper-backed vinyl.* Paper-backed vinyl has a vinyl top layer with a paper rather than fabric backing. This makes the wall covering lighter, so paper-backed vinyl comes prepasted. It's often peelable and washable.

One special type of paper-backed vinyl is expanded vinyl, which has a three-dimensional effect. It's often designed to look like another surface, such as rough plaster, granite, textured paint, or grass cloth. Such materials are especially suitable for walls that aren't perfectly smooth.

■ *Vinyl-coated paper.* This wall covering, made of paper coated with a thin layer of vinyl, looks like paper and not vinyl, so it lends an air of sophistication to light-use areas. Even those vinyl-coated papers that are washable can stain and tear more easily than other papers with vinyl content.

Textiles. Textile wall coverings come in many colors and textures, from very casual to elegantly formal. They're usually made of cotton, linen, other natural plant fibers, or polyester, often bonded to a paper-type backing. Grass cloth is a traditional favorite among textile wall coverings; its threads can be arranged vertically, horizontally, or in a woven pattern.

Hemp, another textile, is similar to grass cloth but has thinner fibers. Wall coverings made of yarn and string (really thin yarn) have been surpassing grass cloth in popularity lately because they're often easier to install.

For a rugged appearance, consider burlap, usually bonded to a backing. At the other end of the spectrum are the sophisticated moiré silks and wall coverings featuring a flame stitch or a pattern printed over the dyed textile.

Some textiles require liner paper underneath; many should be installed only by a skilled paperhanger. Keep in mind that most textiles fray easily and are not washable, though most will accept a spray-on stain repellent. Some are peelable.

Other wallpaper choices. Here are more options in wallpaper materials.

■ *Hand-screened papers.* Each color in a hand-screened paper is applied with a separate handmade and hand-placed silk screen. This process makes hand-screened papers more expensive than the majority of other wallpapers, which are machine printed. Hand-screened papers have a unique three-dimensional appearance and can offer a wealth of colors in just a single pattern. (An example is shown at left.)

Hand-screened patterns match less accurately than machine-printed ones, and edges often need to be trimmed and double-cut at seams. Because these papers are often printed with water-soluble dyes, special care must be taken to keep the printed side free of paste and water. For this reason, professionals usually handle installation.

If you like the appearance of hand-screened paper, you may be able to find some of the new machine-printed papers that have the look of hand-screened ones but are more affordable.

■ *Solid paper.* Whether they're inexpensive or very costly, wall coverings made of solid paper without any vinyl tear easily.

■ *Foils.* Because of their reflective quality, foils and other metallics can brighten up a small, dark space. However, they require an absolutely smooth wall surface and special installation, since they wrinkle easily. Most people have this work done professionally.

■ *Flocked papers.* The texture of a flocked paper resembles damask or cut velvet. Because they're hard to work with, flocks are almost always professionally hung.

■ *Murals.* A mural, often depicting nature or some historic event, opens up a room, particularly if the strips are hung across a large expanse of wall. Or, for a little less drama, try hanging a single-panel mural in the middle of a large wall; on either side hang a paper that matches the mural's background.

In a child's room or a family room, look for photomurals, often scenes taken from nature. In a more elegant setting, try high-quality hand-screened murals, which usually feature traditional European or Oriental themes.

Generally, the panels must be hung in a particular order, as specified by the manufacturer. Be sure to place the panels so that the scene begins at the same height as nearby furniture; otherwise, the scene will appear to "float" above it.

BUYING WALLPAPER

Once you've narrowed down the possibilities, try out your choices at home. Most stores will let you take sample books home, or you can order a larger sample from the manufacturer for a small charge. Prop the book up against the wall, or tape the sample to the wall, and live with it for a while. Or you may want to buy and tack up a single roll.

When you're ready to make your purchase, you'll need to know how many rolls to buy. Be generous when you estimate—rolls printed at a different time may not provide an exact color match, so be sure to order enough the first time.

How many rolls?

To determine how much wallpaper to buy, you need to measure the walls you're covering and take into account any pattern repeat.

Measuring the room. Measure the height and width of each wall (including openings), using a steel tape measure. For a quick and generally reliable estimate of the number of rolls you'll need, use the chart below. The figures assume an 8-foot ceiling. For European rolls, multiply the number of rolls by 1.25. Deduct one roll for every two openings.

Distance around room (in ft.)	Number of rolls for wall	Number of yards for border	Number of rolls for ceiling
30	8	11	2
32	8	12	2
34	10	13	4
36	10	13	4
38	10	14	4
40	10	15	4
42	12	15	4
44	12	16	4
46	12	17	6
48	14	17	6
50	14	18	6
52	14	19	6
54	14	19	6
56	14	20	8
58	16	21	8
60	16	21	8

■ STRAIGHT MATCH & DROP MATCH

In a straight match, design flows directly across strips, so design elements along top of all strips are alike.

With a drop match, pattern at strip's left edge is half a repeat lower than right edge. Top design is alike on alternate strips.

For a more accurate count, multiply the height and width of each wall and add the figures together. Next, deduct 15 square feet for every average-size door or window. For larger or unusually shaped openings, deduct the exact square footage of the opening from your total.

Although rolls vary in width, an American single roll contains 36 square feet of material; a European single roll contains 29 square feet. To allow for cutting and trimming, figure about 30 usable square feet for an American roll, about 25 for a European one.

Divide the total square footage of wall space by 30 (or 25 for European rolls). If you have a fractional remainder, buy an additional roll.

Allowing for pattern repeats. To estimate accurately, you'll also have to consider the wallpaper pattern. With a random pattern, one that doesn't repeat vertically in any regular fashion, simply use the estimating methods described above.

For paper with a straight or drop match (illustrated above), note the repeat height on the back of the sample. Divide the wall height (in inches) by the pattern repeat (in inches); round up any fractional remainder to the next highest number. For example, a 96-inch wall height divided by an 18-inch pattern repeat gives you 5.33 repeats, rounded up to 6.

Then, multiply this number by the length of each repeat to get your "working height." (In our example, 6 repeats multiplied by an 18-inch repeat gives you a working height of 108 inches.)

Figuring your square footage based on working height, rather than actual room height, will yield the number of rolls you need to order.

Estimating for multiple papers. If you're hanging one paper above a chair rail and another below, make an estimate for each paper.

First, figure how many rolls you'd need if you were using only one paper. Then measure the vertical distance each paper will occupy on the wall. Divide this by the total height to get that paper's percentage of the total wall height. Then multiply the total number of rolls you'd need by each percentage to yield the number of rolls of each paper to buy.

For example, say the room would require 11 rolls of one wallpaper. If the wall height is 96 inches and the paper above the chair rail will occupy 57 inches, this paper would cover about 60 percent of the wall. Multiplying 11 rolls times .60 equals 6.6 rolls, or 7 rolls rounded up. For the paper below the chair rail, multiply 11 times .40 to get 4.4 rolls, or 5 rolls rounded up.

Estimating for borders. To estimate for borders, measure the width (in feet) of all areas you're covering. Divide by 3 to get the number of yards needed. Borders usually come in rolls 5 yards long. If you're planning to miter corners around doors and windows, add some extra.

Inspecting your wallpaper

As soon as your wall covering arrives, inspect it carefully. First, check that the pattern numbers are correct and are the same on all the rolls. Every roll should also have the same run, or dye-lot, number.

Then carefully unroll each roll and inspect its entire length. Flaws to look for include uneven ink, wrinkled edges, and poor registration (when colors don't fall within their outlines in the design). Lay two rolls next to each other on a table—the pattern on the left edge of one roll should match the pattern on the right edge of another.

If you find any problems, talk with your dealer right away. If the problem is small and the pattern is in limited supply, you may be able to figure out a way to work around the flaw.

Store your wallpaper in a dry area (a closet usually provides better conditions than a garage) until you're ready to hang it. To avoid wrinkles, lay the rolls horizontally rather than on end, and be sure not to place anything heavy on top of them.

Wallpapering Terms

Bolt. Two or more continuous rolls of wallpaper in a single package.

Booking. Relaxing a pasted strip by folding pasted sides together so the ends overlap and the edges align.

Border. A decorative wallpaper strip, most commonly used to trim a wall at the ceiling line, at chair-rail height, or around doors and windows.

Butt seam. A method of seaming two wallpaper strips by pushing their edges together firmly.

Double-cut seam. A method of seaming two wallpaper strips by overlapping their edges and cutting through both strips.

Drop match. A pattern in which the design element at one edge of a strip is half a repeat lower than at the other edge. The design elements at the top are alike on every other strip.

Lap seam. A method of seaming two strips of wallpaper by overlapping one edge over another.

Liner paper. Blank paper stock hung under wallpaper in order to smooth wall surfaces, absorb excess moisture, and provide a breathable layer between a nonporous wall covering and the wall.

Nonporous wall covering. A wall covering that water or water-soluble adhesive cannot penetrate. Foils and papers with vinyl content are examples of nonporous wall coverings.

Pattern repeat. The vertical distance between one design element on a pattern and the next occurrence of that design element.

Peelable wallpaper. Wallpaper that can be removed from the wall by peeling off the top layer. This leaves a thin residue of paper and adhesive, which is removable with water.

Porous wall covering. A wall covering that water or water-soluble adhesive can penetrate. Most textiles and papers without vinyl are examples.

Prepasted wallpaper. Wallpaper that has been factory-coated with water-soluble adhesive. You activate the paste by soaking the paper in water for the time recommended by the manufacturer.

Pretrimmed wallpaper. Wallpaper from which the selvage edge has been trimmed at the factory.

Random match. A pattern or texture having no design elements that need to be matched between adjoining strips.

Run, or dye-lot, number. The number given to each separate printing of a pattern. Each printing can vary in color and intensity.

Scrubbable wall covering. A wall covering durable enough to be scrubbed with a soft brush and mild soap.

Selvage. The unpatterned side edge of wallpaper that protects it during shipping and handling. The selvage must be trimmed before the wallpaper is hung.

Size, also sizing. A liquid coating applied to wall surfaces to seal the surface, help the adhesive grip the wall, and allow the installer to move the wallpaper into position more easily.

Straight match. A pattern in which the design flows directly across the strips, so the design elements at the top of adjoining matched strips are the same on both strips.

Strip. A length of wallpaper cut to fit.

Strippable wallpaper. Wallpaper that can be removed from the wall by hand without tearing or leaving any paper residue. (It may leave some adhesive.)

Washable wallpaper. Wallpaper that can be cleaned with a solution of mild soap and water.

Preparing the Surface

As with many home improvement projects, success with wallpapering depends in large part on how well you do your "prep" work. Taking the time that's necessary to prepare your walls for wallpaper—making sure they're clean and smooth—will help make the actual work of putting up the paper go quickly and easily.

The steps you'll need to follow depend on the condition of your walls and the material that covers them.

Protecting furnishings

Before you begin, remove as many of the furnishings as you can from the room. Cover the flooring and any remaining furniture with drop cloths. For extra floor protection, you can place towels underneath the drop cloths near the outer edges and then tape the cloths to the top of the baseboards. Don't use newspapers for protection—the ink may come off on damp wall coverings.

You'll also want to take everything off the walls, including any drapery rods. Before removing any wall sconces or electrical faceplates, turn off the power to the room.

If you need to paint woodwork or adjoining walls, complete the painting before you begin wallpapering; let the paint dry thoroughly. You can install any new flooring except carpeting before wallpapering. Carpeting goes down when you've finished working on the walls.

Gathering equipment

To prepare most walls, you'll need a ladder, a sander or sanding block, and 50-grit sandpaper. To clean the walls, you'll want to have sponges, a bucket, and trisodium phosphate (TSP) or ammonia. You'll probably also need primer-sealer.

If you're removing existing wallpaper, have on hand a 4- or 6-inch broad knife, a trash can, and towels. Also, locate a steamer or a canister-style garden sprayer (available from a tool rental

company), a sponge, or a short-handled mop. You'll also need sandpaper, a saw, or a scarifying tool. Wallpaper removal enzyme may be helpful.

Preparing a papered wall

If your walls are already wallpapered, it's usually best to remove the paper before applying the new wall covering. Even when an existing wall covering looks good, professionals usually recommend removing it because moisture from the paste used to apply the new wallpaper can loosen paper that's been holding well, spoiling the new covering.

If your old wallpaper is in good condition, smooth in texture, and only one layer thick, and the new wallpaper is porous, you may hang over the existing paper. If, when you start removing the old paper, the process damages the surface of the wall, you'll have no choice but to paper over the old wallpaper.

Removing old wallpaper. How you remove the old wallpaper will depend on the kind of paper that's on your walls.

Strippable paper is the easiest to remove, since you can pull both the vinyl coating and the backing off the wall in one easy step. Starting at a seam, you simply pull the paper off gently and slowly at an angle that allows you to keep both hands near the wall. With peelable paper, you follow the same procedure to pull off the vinyl coating, but the fabric or paper backing remains on the wall.

To remove the backing, and to remove other wall coverings that aren't strippable or peelable, you'll have to rewet the adhesive that holds them to the wall. Only when the paste is wet can you pull the paper off the wall.

Tips for Novices

No doubt you've heard stories about people who, after wallpapering for the first time, vowed never to do it again. Often, beginners think that a small room will be easier to paper than a large one, so they start with the bathroom. In fact, a bathroom is one of the hardest areas to paper because of its confined space and the presence of so many corners, fixtures, and pipes.

If you're a novice paperhanger, here are some guidelines you can follow to ensure that your first experience will be a pleasant and successful one.

■ Choose an area with as few obstructions and corners as possible, such as a single wall or an entry hall.

■ For ease in cutting and in matching patterns at seams, select wallpaper with a random or straight match, not a drop match.

■ Choose an open, airy pattern so that the background color, rather than a design, predominates at edges.

■ Buy high-quality, machine-printed, pretrimmed paper. You won't have to cut off selvages or deal with paper that wrinkles easily.

■ Consider using prepasted paper with some vinyl content (such as paper-backed vinyl) for your first project.

■ Be sure to use primer-sealer on the walls before hanging the paper. With primer-sealer, the paper will adhere more readily to the wall.

■ If you're renting or buying tools from your wallpaper dealer, make sure you know how to use them correctly.

■ Set up a large, smooth, clean pasting table and, if possible, work with a partner.

If your paper has a nonpeelable, nonporous covering, such as vinyl or foil, moisture applied to the surface can't soak through to the adhesive. For this reason, you'll have to create "openings," as shown below, using coarse sandpaper, a saw (scrape its entire blade against the wallpaper surface in many places), or a scarifying tool (available through your wallpaper retailer).

Once the peeling or scraping exposes a porous surface, you're ready to soak the adhesive. One method is to use a steamer, which converts water to steam that runs through a hose to a pan with a trigger; you move the pan slowly along the wall so steam can penetrate the covering (see illustration below, center).

Another popular method is to spray the wall with a canister-style garden sprayer filled with very hot water; adjust the nozzle to a fine spray when you're working close to surfaces not being stripped. You may want to add a liquid enzyme to the water to help break down the adhesive; if you do, ventilate the room well and wear gloves.

For a simpler approach, just wet the wall with a sponge or short-handled mop dipped into a bucket of very hot water (with enzyme, if you like).

Wet one wall at a time, or only as much wall surface as you can keep wet and work on before it dries out. Apply moisture, let it soak in, and then rewet the surface before it dries. You may have to wet the wall several times—the paper should be as wet as a soaked jar label ready to peel off. (This can take up to 15 minutes.)

Working down from the top of the wall, scrape off the wallpaper with a broad knife; be careful not to chip or otherwise damage the surface. If the paper doesn't pull away easily, wet it again.

Removing multiple layers of wallpaper usually works best if you tackle one layer at a time. If you find any nonporous layers, be sure to sand or score them before wetting them down.

Because old adhesive may show through new light-colored wallpaper, you may want to remove all remaining old adhesive by more soaking and scraping, or by sanding.

Repair any cracks, holes, or other wall damage (for help, turn to pages 38–40); make the surface as smooth as possible. Then wash the wall from the bottom up with a solution of trisodium phosphate or ammonia and water. After allowing the wall to dry thoroughly, apply primer-sealer.

When you don't remove old wallpaper. If you decide not to remove the old wallpaper, or if removal is damaging the walls, you'll need to prepare the papered surface to receive the new wall covering. If you've been applying water or steam, allow the wall to dry thoroughly (about 12 hours) before proceeding.

Repaste and roll any loose seams; then spackle and sand all nicks, rough spots, and overlapped seams. Starting at the bottom, wash the wall with a solution of trisodium phosphate or ammonia and water and let it dry completely.

To check whether your old paper will "bleed" ink through your new wall covering, moisten a small piece of the old paper with a clean sponge. If any ink comes off on the sponge, the existing paper could discolor the new covering. To prevent this, apply a special primer-sealer formulated to seal stains.

If the existing paper is nonporous, use vinyl-to-vinyl primer. This will ensure proper drying of the adhesive and prevent mildew.

Preparing other surfaces

Most surfaces are easier to prepare than previously papered walls. However, uneven surfaces need special attention.

Painted walls. Scrape and sand painted walls until they're smooth; then dust. To degloss surfaces, you can use sandpaper or an extra-strong solution of trisodium phosphate or ammonia and water. Repair and wash the wall as described under wallpaper removal at left. Let the surface dry. Apply primer-sealer unless the paint is alkyd.

New plaster walls. Before papering, you'll have to wait until the new plas-

■ REMOVING OLD WALLPAPER

Using sandpaper and working in several directions across wall, score surface of nonporous wallpaper in many places.

Wet one wall at a time, using a steamer, as shown, or a sprayer, sponge, or mop, until surface is thoroughly soaked.

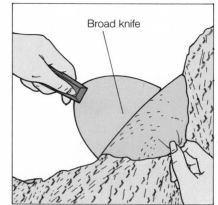

Broad knife

Starting at top and working down, remove old wallpaper with a broad knife. Rewet wall to remove any adhesive residue.

ter has thoroughly dried. This can take from 1 to 4 months; consult your contractor for the time. Wash the new plaster with vinegar to neutralize it. Then apply two coats of primer-sealer.

New wallboard. All wallboard joints should be taped, spackled, and sanded. Then dust with a short-napped soft brush. A slightly damp sponge will remove the last particles of dust. Then apply primer-sealer.

Uneven surfaces. When used on walls, such materials as cinder block, concrete, wood paneling, textured plaster, and textured paint can be uneven enough that you'll have to smooth them before wallpapering.

To check whether a wall's roughness will be a problem, apply adhesive to a piece of the new wall covering, smooth it on the wall, and look at it. If surface roughness shows through the paper, you'll have to smooth the wall. (Remove the scrap before it dries.)

For light to moderate unevenness, or for a small area, you can apply nonshrinking spackle or tape compound. When it's completely dry, sand it and apply primer-sealer. You can also smooth the surface by hanging liner paper; consult your dealer for the best weight paper to use. Hang it vertically if you're sure the seams won't fall where the wallpaper seams will go; otherwise, hang the liner paper horizontally, as shown at right.

More significant unevenness calls for plastering the surface, a job for a professional.

Treating mildew

Moist areas, such as bathrooms and outer walls, are often susceptible to mildew stains. If you see mildew, you need to remove not just the stains but the underlying mildew itself.

Mildew is primarily caused by a fungus living on damp, organic material. To kill the fungus and remove stains, scrub the walls with liquid bleach or a solution of half bleach and half water.

Then wash the walls with a solution of trisodium phosphate and water; rinse well. Let the washed surface

dry completely (at least 24 hours). Finally, apply a coat of alkyd (oil-base) primer-sealer into which you have mixed a commercially available fungicide additive.

To prevent mildew from reappearing, choose a fairly thick wallpaper. You can also use ready-mixed clay-base adhesive if it's appropriate for your wallpaper; add a fungicide to the adhesive. If possible, install a good fan and more effective window openings to provide adequate ventilation.

Priming & sizing

Thorough surface preparation often involves applying primer-sealer to help coverings adhere to the wall. In some cases, size is also used to aid adhesion.

Priming. In general, wallpaper goes on more easily if you've applied primer-sealer to the wall. Primer-sealer keeps the surface from absorbing moisture from the adhesive, allowing the paper to adhere more readily. It also protects the wall from damage when the covering is removed later on.

Some clean walls painted with a high-quality flat alkyd paint may not need a primer.

Choose a primer-sealer specifically designed as an undercoat for wall coverings. Using a roller, apply it at least 24 hours before hanging the wall

covering so the wall will be thoroughly dry (follow the manufacturer's directions regarding drying time).

Some professionals believe that alkyd primer-sealers bond to walls better than water-soluble acrylics. Acrylic primer-sealers, however, are easier to use and clean up. You'll want to use alkyds in high-moisture areas, over an alkyd paint, or if recommended by the wallpaper manufacturer.

When you're hanging a semi-transparent paper over existing wallpaper or over a colored wall, use pigmented primer-sealer. You can also have the primer mixed to match the paper's background color, so any hairline seam cracks will be less obvious.

Sizing. Size is a liquid coating applied to the wall to make paper adhere better and go on more easily. In most cases, today's primer-sealers make the use of size unnecessary.

However, you may want to consider using size if you're hanging a porous or heavy paper, if the wall is textured or has an alkyd painted surface, if the paper or seams aren't sticking well, or if the wall-covering manufacturer recommends it.

Use a roller or brush to apply size. It dries quickly, so you can usually begin hanging the wall covering immediately, unless the wall-covering manufacturer recommends otherwise.

■ HOW TO HANG LINER PAPER

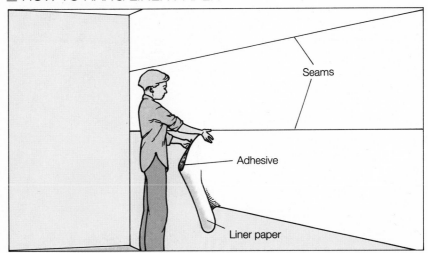

Use liner paper over rough surfaces. (It's also recommended under some textiles.) To be sure seams won't fall in same place as those of wall covering, hang liner paper horizontally.

Hanging Wallpaper

Proper equipment, good preparation and layout, and careful cutting, pasting, and hanging are the building blocks to a successful wallpapering job. All of these, plus a great deal of patience, will help transform a plain room into an attractive and appealing living space.

Read through the following pages to familiarize yourself with the basics of hanging wallpaper. Also, review the manufacturer's instructions that came with your wallpaper. If you have additional questions, ask your dealer.

Try to work during daylight hours; you'll match patterns better and see seams more accurately than at night. Stop when you get tired; cover any wet rolls and tools with plastic and place them in the refrigerator overnight.

If you're hanging a border paper either alone or with companion paper, information on layout and hanging begins on page 92. Note that if you're planning to paper the ceiling, you'll need to do it before you paper the walls; for directions, turn to page 91.

BASIC TECHNIQUES

Here are the basic procedures you need to follow to hang wallpaper. Take your time; attention to detail and careful work will ensure a perfect job.

Equipment for wallpapering

Keep handy the stepladder, drop cloths, bucket, and sponges (good-quality, natural ones) you used for preparing the surface. If you're papering a ceiling, use two sturdy ladders and set up an extension plank between them.

The specialized tools you'll need just for hanging are illustrated at left.

■ *Measuring.* It's essential to have a plumb bob or long carpenter's level for vertical lines; you may also want a short level for small spaces and for checking the straightness of the paper as you work. Measure the room with a steel tape measure.

■ *Cutting.* For cutting paper, you'll need a razor knife, preferably the type with snap-off blades. This knife allows you to change blades easily, a job you'll be doing frequently. Also have on hand a metal straightedge and large utility shears.

To help trim paper edges straight after hanging, you'll want a 4- or 6-inch broad knife (the narrower blade allows more control).

■ *Pasting.* To paste paper, you can use a short-napped paint roller with a paint tray or a pasting brush with a bucket. A whisk works well for mixing dry paste. For prepasted paper, you'll need a water tray.

■ TOOLS FOR HANGING WALLPAPER

Wallpapering tools include (1) natural sponge, (2) seam roller, (3) tape measure, (4) short-napped paint roller, (5) carpenter's level, (6) metal straightedge, (7) smoothing brush, (8) wallpaper smoother, (9) razor or utility knife, (10) broad knife, (11) plumb bob, (12) water tray.

Set up a pasting table—a long table, boards on sawhorses, or a table rented from your dealer. Some people use a stand near the table for the paste. A large plastic bag is handy for booking strips.

Walls, seams, and borders may each require a different adhesive. The correct choice depends on the type of wallpaper you're hanging, so check the manufacturer's recommendations. If you have a choice, you'll find premixed adhesive easier to work with than dry. Clay-base adhesive is tackier and holds to the wall better than cellulose or wheat-base paste, but it can be messier and more difficult to handle.

If your wall covering contains vinyl, you'll also want a tube of vinyl-to-vinyl seam adhesive. It's packaged for easy application at overlapping seams, which occur at corners.

To hang a border over a vinyl paper, you may need vinyl-to-vinyl adhesive in tub form. Some professionals use this paste even when they're installing a prepasted border over a coordinated vinyl wall covering.

■ *Smoothing.* To smooth wallpaper, use a wallpaper smoother, a good-quality smoothing brush, a rag, or a sponge. The tool you choose should let you apply pressure evenly, yet feel whether the wallpaper is smooth or uneven. With textured or embossed paper, use the smoothing brush.

A seam roller presses seams firmly to the wall; the beveled type may make seams less noticeable.

Layout

Before you cut your first strip, think about where you'll hang your first and last strips and how you'll hang around obstacles. Solving potential problems ahead of time, rather than while you're holding long strips of wet wallpaper, will result in less wasted paper and fewer headaches during the hanging process.

Since the pattern on the last strip you hang probably won't match the pattern of the strip it meets, you may want to choose your end point first. Look for the least conspicuous place in the room; usually, it's over a door or in a corner near the entrance.

■ PLANNING PROPER LAYOUT

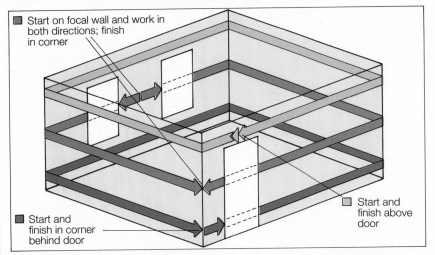

■ Start on focal wall and work in both directions; finish in corner

■ Start and finish in corner behind door

■ Start and finish above door

Most rooms have several possible start and end points for hanging wallpaper. Plan to end in an inconspicuous spot; start in the same spot or at a focal point. Then check each possible layout for seam placement all around room.

Then locate a good starting point—it may be the same as your end point. Or you can start at the room's focal point, a fireplace or large window, for example, and work in both directions toward the end point. At the focal point, you can center either a strip or a seam. The sample layout above shows several possible start and end points.

Taking one possible layout, determine where the seams will fall by holding a roll of your wall covering where the first strip will hang. Note where the edges rest. Flip the roll end over end to find the next seam location. Continue to work your way all around the room.

Try to avoid having seams fall closer than 4 inches to such obstacles as corners, windows, and doors. That kind of placement wastes paper, and narrow pieces may not adhere well to the wall. Also, you'll want a seam near the center of any fixture so you can fit the paper around it without having to cut a long slit.

If seams fall in awkward spots, pick another starting point and work your way around again; each room usually has several possible starting places. If you're starting and ending in the same spot, you can alter the location of the seams by making your starting strip narrower. (Make a vertical cut along the side of the strip that will adjoin the last strip.)

When you decide on start and end points, mark them on the wall.

If you're installing two papers of different widths with a chair rail or border in between, do a separate layout for each one.

Establishing plumb

Because most house walls are not plumb (perfectly vertical), you'll need to establish a plumb line and use it to align the first strip. You'll also need to establish a plumb line every time you turn a corner.

Begin by adding ¼ inch to the width of your wallpaper. Measure this distance from your starting point and mark the wall near the ceiling. (The offset avoids the possibility that the chalk or pencil used to make the plumb line will bleed through the seam.)

To draw a plumb line, you can use either a plumb bob or a carpenter's level.

Plumb bob. Rub light-colored chalk along a plumb bob string or another string with a weight. Place a tack in the wall at the mark you just made and tie the string's end to the tack so the point of the plumb bob or weight dangles just a fraction of an inch above the baseboard.

Once the weight stops swinging back and forth, press the lower end of

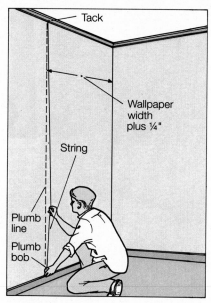

To use a plumb bob, measure out width of paper plus ¼ inch, and mark wall. Snap string at mark.

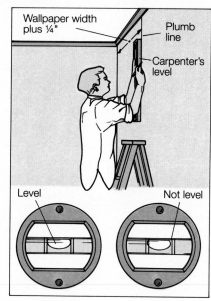

To use a carpenter's level, draw line down wall, starting at mark. Bubble in level must be centered for line to be plumb (see inset).

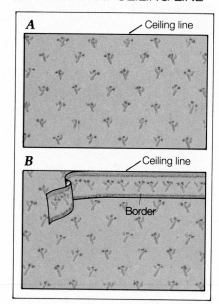

Full design element should fall just below ceiling line (A). With a border, place paper so border won't chop design (B).

the string against the wall. Pull out on the middle of the line until it's taut, as shown above, and then let go. The vertical chalk mark left on the wall is the plumb line.

Carpenter's level. Hold a carpenter's level vertically on the wall, placing one edge against the mark you made. Adjust the level until the bubble that designates plumb is centered. Draw a line in light pencil along the level's edge. Move the level down and repeat, connecting lines until you have a floor-to-ceiling plumb line.

Make sure that you hold the level steady and that the bubble remains absolutely level, as illustrated above, center; even a slight variance will cause problems in hanging your wallpaper plumb. To be sure your level is accurate, use a plumb bob to check the first line you draw.

Cutting the paper

For visually pleasing results, any design in the wall covering should look nice at the ceiling line.

To avoid chopping the design in an awkward spot, plan to have a full design element fall just below the ceil-ing line, as shown above, at right. If you can keep a plain background area at the top edge, any variations in ceiling height won't affect the design. For wallpaper with a drop match, place two pieces on a table, match them, and then use a straightedge to find the best breaking point across both strips.

If you're planning to hang a border over wallpaper, you'll want to take into account how much of the paper's design the border will cover. Lay the border over the wall covering on a table so the desired top design element in the wall covering starts below the border. Then lightly mark the wall covering at the top edge of the border. This mark indicates where to place the paper at the ceiling line.

If your design includes a chair rail, you may need to compromise between the pattern appearance at ceiling height and at chair-rail height.

To cut a strip, measure the wall length needed. On the wallpaper roll, locate the design element you want at the top edge, measure 2 inches above that, and cut across the paper with a razor knife and straightedge. Or make a straight crease at that point, keeping the edges aligned as you fold, and cut along the crease with utility shears.

Then measure the length of paper you need, add 4 inches, and make the bottom cut. Roll the strip bottom to top, pattern side out.

At first, cut—and hang—one strip at a time. As you develop confidence, and if your paper has a random match or a straight match with a short repeat, you can cut several strips in a row. (Be sure to number them lightly in pencil on the back.) Cut only enough strips to reach the next obstacle, such as a window or corner.

When you're cutting subsequent strips for a drop match, the best way to ensure that the pattern matches is to hold the roll up to the wall. Leaving a minimum 2-inch top allowance, match the pattern to the adjoining strip and make a crease 2 inches above that match. After placing the roll on the table, make the top cut at the crease. Measure the wall length plus 4 inches and then make the bottom cut.

Pasting & booking

With some wall coverings, you'll need to apply adhesive to the backing before hanging. Prepasted papers already have an adhesive backing, so all that's required is a soaking in water to activate the paste. Both methods usually require that the papers be booked, a special folding method that allows the paper to relax while it absorbs the adhesive.

Although prepasted papers technically are already pasted, some professional paperhangers repaste them before they're hung. When prepasted paper first appeared, some rolls had uneven, unreliable coatings of paste, so many professionals repasted the paper to avoid problems.

Although manufacturing techniques have improved since then, some installers still recommend repasting, claiming that it increases adhesion and reduces shrinkage. Repasting also makes it easier to move the booked paper around on the wall.

On the other hand, repasting prepasted paper voids the manufacturer's warranty and eliminates strippability. Some dealers warn that the added paste may occasionally react adversely with the paste already applied to the paper, leading to adhesion problems and chemical spotting.

Discuss the pros and cons of repasting prepasted paper with your dealer. If you decide to repaste, follow the directions for pasting unpasted paper, except dilute the adhesive with 50 percent more water than for unpasted paper. Use a short-napped roller to apply the adhesive.

Pasting unpasted paper. The instructions that come with your wallpaper are the best guide to choosing the proper adhesive for your wall covering. Premixed adhesives are convenient and easy to use. If you're using a dry adhesive, mix it according to the manufacturer's directions until it's smooth and not too thick; the consistency should be like gravy. Squish any lumps.

Place the strip, pattern side down, on the pasting table. To apply the adhesive, use either a roller with a short-napped cover or a pasting brush. If you're using the roller, work from the center of the strip to the edges, as shown below, at left, making sure the edges are well pasted. With the brush, apply the paste in a figure-8 pattern.

Cover the back of the wallpaper completely and smoothly; aim for a thin, even coat. Try not to get any paste on the pattern side. After hanging a strip or so, you'll get the feel of the right amount of paste to use. If the strip won't stick, you're not using enough; if paste oozes out, you're using too much. On a hot, dry day, using a bit more paste keeps it from drying too fast.

Then book the paper, as described at right.

Soaking prepasted paper. Place a water tray on a towel on the floor next to your work table. Align the tray so its long side is parallel with the side of the table. Fill the tray two-thirds full of lukewarm water.

First, immerse the loosely rolled strip in the water for 10 to 15 seconds (or as recommended by the manufacturer). Then, grasping the top corners of the soaked strip, pull it up slowly, about one foot per second, letting any excess water fall back into the tray (see illustration below, center).

Finally, place the strip, pattern side down, on the table and book as described below, unless the manufacturer recommends against booking. (If you're not booking your paper, you can place the water tray on the floor directly beneath the wall area the strip will cover.)

Booking. To promote even adhesion, wallpaper needs time before it's hung to absorb the paste. Moistened paper also expands slightly; if it's hung too quickly, the paper expands on the wall, causing bubbling. To let the strip relax, you book the paper. Most wallpapers, except foils and a few others, require booking.

Begin by folding the bottom third of the strip over the middle, pasted sides together, as shown below; take care not to crease the wallpaper at the fold. Edges should align neatly. Then

■ PASTING A STRIP

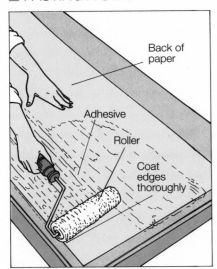

With unpasted paper, apply adhesive with a roller, working from center of strip to edges. Be sure edges are well coated.

■ SOAKING A STRIP

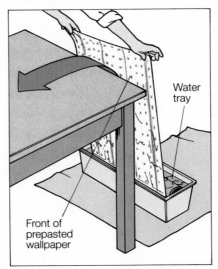

With prepasted paper, immerse strip in water for time recommended by manufacturer. Using both hands, lift out slowly.

■ BOOKING A STRIP

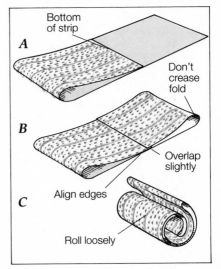

To book, fold lower third over middle, aligning edges (A); fold over remaining portion just to overlap end (B). Roll loosely (C).

fold over the remaining portion of the strip until it overlaps the bottom cut end slightly, again aligning the edges neatly.

If you have pretrimmed paper, you're ready to roll the strip loosely, place it in a large plastic bag, and close the bag. (This creates an evenly humid environment in which the paper can relax without drying out.)

If you need to trim your paper, check that the edges are precisely aligned. On one side, line up a straight-edge with the trim marks. Using a razor knife, cut through both layers. Turn the strip around and follow the same procedure for the opposite side. Then roll and enclose in a bag as for pre-trimmed paper.

After waiting the booking time recommended by the manufacturer, usually 5 to 15 minutes, you're ready to hang your first strip. (Remember not to cut the second strip until the first one is hung.) While you're waiting, you can clean the pasting table with a damp sponge. Dry your hands before continuing.

Hanging the first strip

With your stepladder positioned next to the plumb line on the wall, unroll the first booked strip but don't unfold it. Then, holding the strip by the upper corners, slowly unfold the top portion, letting the rest of the strip fall down. (Refer to the illustrated hanging sequence that appears on the facing page as you work.)

Allowing the strip to overlap the ceiling line by about 2 inches, place the top portion of the edge close to but not on the plumb line. Then press the strip to the wall at the ceiling line just hard enough that the paper sticks to the wall without falling down.

Next, adjust the paper until the side edge is perfectly parallel with the plumb line, picking up the strip as needed but being careful not to stretch the paper. If necessary, move the top corners so the paper hangs without wrinkles.

Using a smoother and fanning out from the seam, gently smooth the top portion of the strip so the paper, adhesive, and wall make firm contact. Re-

member to smooth the paper into the ceiling edge as well.

Unfold the rest of the strip, aligning and smoothing it as you did the top portion. When the entire strip is straight and smooth, run a seam roller or sponge along the edge that will not meet the next strip.

To trim the ceiling and baseboard edges, use a razor knife, keeping a broad knife between the razor blade and the wall covering to ensure a straight cut and to protect the paper. To insure smooth cuts, don't move both the broad knife and the razor knife at the same time. Change blades often, especially if you're hanging a textile. (Some textile manufacturers recommend that you do edge trimming only after the material has dried.)

Wipe excess adhesive from the wall covering, ceiling, and baseboard with a clean, damp sponge; rinse the sponge often. Before continuing with the next strip, clean and dry your hands.

Hanging the second strip

When you hang the second strip, you'll create a seam where this strip meets the first one. In most situations, a butt seam is the best way to join two strips of wallpaper, since it's the least noticeable. But some wall coverings, such as hand-screened papers and some textiles, require double-cut seams.

Although harder to do than butt seams, double-cut seams eliminate any gaps between strips. Double-cutting also comes in handy when you're working around wall irregularities.

Sometimes, textiles need reverse-strip hanging, which yields better-looking results when rolls are not dyed evenly. Simply alternate the strips as you paper around the room: if the first strip was hung with the first cut end at the ceiling, hang the second strip with the first cut end at the floor.

Prepare the second strip and hang, following the directions for the seam you're using.

Butt seam. Unfold the top portion of the second strip on the wall, as you did for the first one. With one hand, work from the top down to align the second strip with the first, spreading your fingers broadly to create even pressure. Move your hand firmly but gently, trying to move not just the edge but the entire strip.

Use the other hand to hold as much of the strip as possible off the wall so you can align the edge without stretching the wallpaper, as shown below, at left. When the edge of the top portion of the strip butts tightly to the adjoining strip, unfold the rest of the strip and finish aligning the seam. Then smooth the strip and trim along the ceiling line and baseboard; wipe clean.

(Continued on page 86)

■ MAKING A BUTT SEAM

Matching any pattern, align second strip with first, positioning paper with spread fingers. Do not stretch paper.

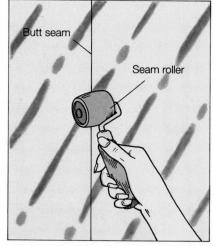

When seam is straight and tight and adhesive is tacky, use a seam roller to roll seam lightly.

HANGING THE FIRST STRIP

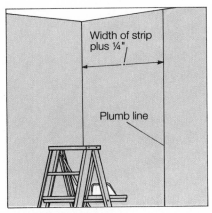

1 Draw a plumb line on wall for first strip. Position stepladder next to plumb line so you can reach top of wall. Place tools nearby for easy access.

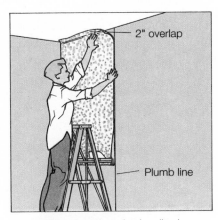

2 Unfold top portion of strip, allowing remainder to fall. Lightly press strip to wall so edge is next to but not on plumb line and top overlaps ceiling line 2 inches.

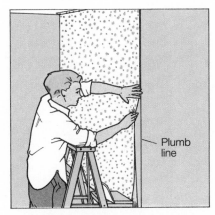

3 Spreading fingers broadly over strip, gently move top of strip until it's parallel with and right beside plumb line. Pick up strip as needed; avoid stretching it.

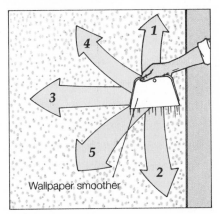

4 To smooth paper, fan out from midpoint of aligned seam with a smoother, using stroke order shown. Paper, adhesive, and wall must make firm contact.

5 Smooth paper tightly where wall and ceiling meet by running a seam roller or wallpaper smoother along top where ceiling or molding begins.

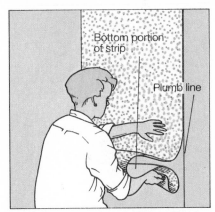

6 Carefully unfold remainder of strip; align parallel with plumb line. Smooth this section as you did top portion. Make sure entire strip is smooth and straight.

7 To make sure seam lies flat, run a seam roller or sponge along edge that won't abut next strip. Do not roll other edge of strip yet.

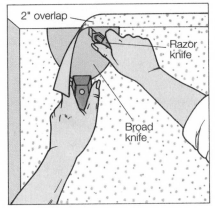

8 Using a razor knife and keeping a broad knife between it and wall, carefully trim excess paper from top and bottom of strip. Move only one tool at a time.

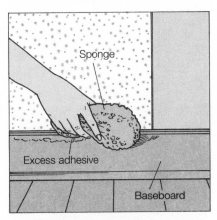

9 Dip a clean sponge in lukewarm water and wring. Use sponge to wipe excess adhesive off wall covering, baseboard, and ceiling. Clean sponge after each use.

Wallpaper **85**

■ MAKING A DOUBLE-CUT SEAM

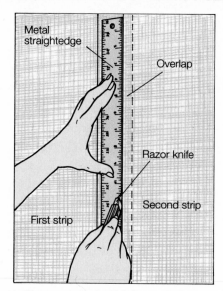

Letting second strip slightly overlap first one, match any pattern. With a razor knife, cut through both strips within overlap area.

Remove top scrap piece (A). Carefully lift strip just enough to remove scrap underneath (B). Smooth and trim; roll seam.

Finally, after checking that the seam is lying flat, roll it using light pressure, particularly if you're hanging a textile.

Double-cut seam. Unfold, tack, and align the second strip as for a butt seam, except let the second strip slightly overlap the first, as shown above. If appropriate, match the pattern. Using a razor knife, slice through both strips, being careful not to cut into the surface of the wall. Carefully lift off the scrap from the second strip; then, lifting the second strip just a bit, remove the scrap underneath. Reposition the strip and smooth. Trim the top and bottom edges and roll the seam.

Covering corners

Wallpapering around inside and outside corners requires special attention, especially because walls may not be plumb.

Inside corners. Pushing a strip of wallpaper into an inside corner and then continuing that strip on the next wall can result in puckered, crooked paper. Instead, it's best to split the strip and hang some on each wall, as shown below.

First, measure from the preceding strip to the corner at three different heights. Then cut the strip vertically ¼ inch wider than the widest measurement; don't discard the leftover paper. After pasting and booking the strip, butt it to the preceding one and smooth it firmly into and around the corner. To help the strip lie flat in the corner, snip the overlaps at the top and bottom as shown.

Measure the width of the leftover piece of wallpaper. From the corner, measure that same distance plus ¼ inch on the adjacent wall and make a plumb line. Paste and book the strip.

Position the strip's uncut edge next to but not on the plumb line; let the edge in the corner overlap the previous piece ¼ inch. (With a nonporous

■ WALLPAPERING AROUND INSIDE CORNERS

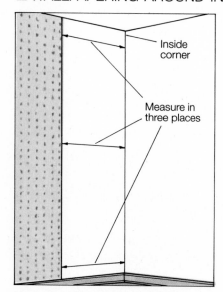

Measure from strip edge to corner in three places. Add ¼ inch to largest measurement; cut next strip vertically to that width.

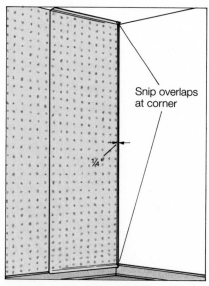

Butt strip to previous one and smooth into and around corner. Snip top and bottom overlaps at corner so strip lies flat.

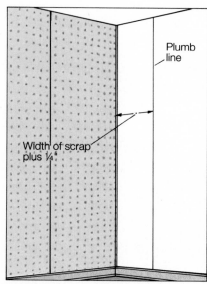

From corner, hang a plumb line at a distance equal to width of scrap plus ¼ inch. Align scrap to line; overlap ¼ inch in corner.

wall covering, use a vinyl-to-vinyl adhesive on the overlap.) This overlap, called a lap seam, allows you to make the paper on the second wall plumb. Any pattern misalignment at the seam is usually not noticeable.

Outside corners. To hang around an outside corner, butt and smooth the new strip to the previous one, snip the top and bottom overlaps at the corner, and smooth the strip, as shown at right.

Drop a plumb line on the new wall at a distance equal to the width of the next strip plus ½ inch. Then measure the distance between the plumb line and the edge of the corner strip at several heights. If the measurements are the same, the new wall is plumb and you can hang the next strip as for a straight wall.

For a wall that's only slightly out of plumb, you can use a technique, shown at far right, that minimizes pattern mismatch at the corner. If the dis-

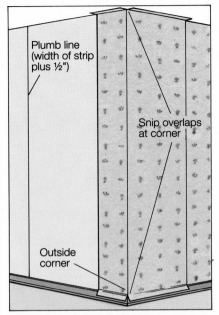

Plumb line (width of strip plus ½")

Snip overlaps at corner

Outside corner

Smooth strip tightly to first wall. Snip overlaps at corner; then smooth around corner and onto next wall. Drop a new plumb line.

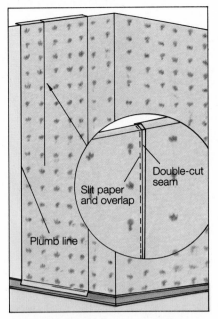

Double-cut seam

Slit paper and overlap

Plumb line

If next wall isn't exactly plumb, slit paper; align to previous strip and plumb line, overlapping at slit. Double-cut slit (see inset).

Solving Common Problems

Typical problems you may encounter when hanging wallpaper include those listed below. Some can be prevented by careful pasting and hanging; others need to be dealt with as you go.

Unplumb surfaces. As you work around the room, you may find that the pattern doesn't always match at seam lines or that design elements at the top look crooked compared with the ceiling edge. Your difficulty probably stems from the fact that your walls and ceilings are not plumb.

In general, hanging the wallpaper straight (along a plumb line) helps overall appearance more than having the pattern match exactly. With a boldly patterned paper, however, you may need to favor the pattern break at the ceiling over having the paper plumb. Try to make corrections in inconspicuous

spots. To paper adjoining walls that are not plumb, use the techniques for corners discussed above.

Wrinkles or misalignment. If wallpaper wrinkles or will not butt properly to the adjoining strip, it's probably not aligned correctly at the top. Don't try to stretch or force it. Instead, gently pull off the strip and reposition it on the wall.

Separated seams. If seams pull apart as the adhesive dries, you may have used too much or too little adhesive when pasting, the strip may have dried out after booking, or it may have stretched as you hung it.

Applying a little seam adhesive just under the edges often helps; or use a small brush to apply more adhesive to the backing at the seam edge. Press firmly and wipe away any excess glue.

If the adhesive has already dried, your only solution may be to color the exposed seam area with a special mixture of artist watercolors and pigmented primer-sealer.

Curled edges. When edges curl, it's usually because they haven't been sufficiently pasted or moistened. Pasting the edges well and booking the strips in a plastic bag helps prevent this condition. If it occurs, try the remedies described at left for separated seams.

Air bubbles and lumps. Carefully smoothing the wall covering as you go can help avoid air bubbles. Minor ones usually disappear when the strip is dry. Stubborn air bubbles can be punctured with a razor knife to release trapped air. A broad knife works well for smoothing out any paste lumps.

■ WALLPAPERING AROUND WINDOWS & DOORS

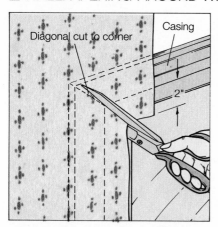

Hang paper over opening, trimming excess paper to within 2 inches of edge of opening. Make diagonal cuts into corners.

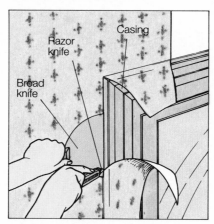

Smooth wallpaper into place. Trim excess around frame with a razor knife, protecting wall covering with a broad knife.

■ WALLPAPERING AROUND RECESSED WINDOWS

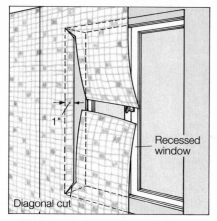

At middle of window, cut horizontally to within 1 inch of edge; then cut vertically, making diagonal cuts into corners.

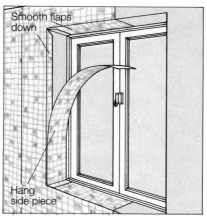

Smooth flaps into place. Matching any pattern, apply side piece, cutting it ¼ inch narrower to prevent fraying.

■ WALLPAPERING AROUND OVERWIDE WINDOWS

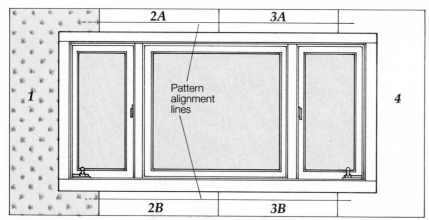

Use a level aligned with design element in strip (1) to mark horizontal line above and below window. Hang strips in pairs (2A and 2B, then 3A and 3B), aligning pattern with line. After hanging next full strip (4), adjust strips to match pattern, if necessary. Then trim.

tance from the plumb line to the previous strip is greater at the top of the wall than at the bottom, slit the next strip partway from the bottom up, working within a background area of the design; slit from the top if the lower distance is greater.

Next, align the near side of this strip with the preceding one and the far side with the plumb line; adjust the length of the cut and overlap the edges of the slit until the strip is smooth and plumb. Then double-cut the overlap.

As an easier alternative to the technique just described, you can simply hang the new strip parallel with the plumb line and use a lap seam where the strips meet.

If a strip ends at an outside corner, cut it back ⅛ to ¼ inch to prevent the paper from fraying and peeling at the corner.

Wallpapering around openings

The procedures for papering around openings, whether they're as large as a door or as small as an electrical receptacle, are variations on those for wallpapering a solid wall.

Doors, windows, and other large openings. Don't try to custom fit large openings by meticulous measurement and advance cutting. Instead, hang the strip as you normally would, but with the following difference: cut the excess material to within 2 inches of where you'll trim, as shown at left, top. Using shears, cut diagonal slits to the corners of the opening.

With a smoother, press the wall covering into place along all edges of the opening. Use a razor knife to trim excess material around the opening's frame, protecting the covering with a broad knife. If the molding is intricate, make scissor snips.

To wallpaper around a recessed window, hang the strip normally, letting it overlap the window. At about the middle of the window, make a horizontal cut to within 1 inch of the window, as shown at left, center.

From this point cut the paper vertically until you can make a diagonal cut into each corner. Smooth the top and bottom flaps and the side piece

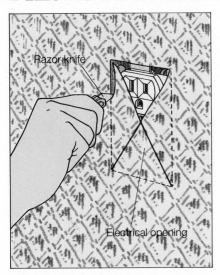

Use a razor knife to make an X-shaped cut over opening from corner to corner. Trim excess along edges of opening.

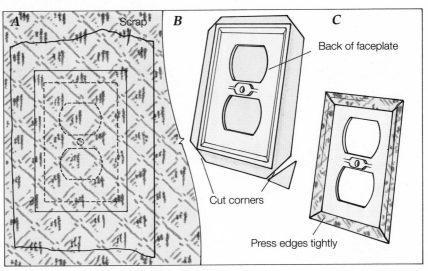

Holding pasted faceplate on wall, position pasted scrap over it so scrap aligns with pattern (A). Holding scrap and faceplate together, place face down on table; trim scrap to within ½ inch of edge, cutting corners (B). Wrap paper around (C) and cut openings.

into place. Install a matched piece to fit the side, cutting it ¼ inch narrower to avoid fraying. Trim all edges. Repeat the process for the other side.

The difficulty of papering around an overwide window is that usually you can't fit a carpenter's level above or below the window to keep the paper plumb. If you have a short level, hold it against the side edge of each strip, adjusting the strip until the bubble is level.

Otherwise, using a carpenter's level, draw horizontal lines across the wall above and below the window from a specific design element in the last strip you hung (see bottom illustration on facing page). Then match the corresponding design element in each strip to this line, hanging the strips in the order shown.

Electrical openings and faceplates. Be sure to turn off the electricity to the room if you haven't already done so. Then remove the faceplate.

Hang the wallpaper as you would normally, letting it cover the opening. Then, using a razor knife, make an X-shaped cut over the opening, extending the cuts into the corners, as shown above. Carefully trim the excess paper around the edges.

For a nice finishing touch, you can cover the faceplate to match the paper

that surrounds it, as shown above. Sand and prime the faceplate. Apply vinyl-to-vinyl adhesive to the right side of the faceplate and to the wrong side of a scrap of wallpaper. Hold the faceplate over the opening, aligning the screw holes. Place the pasted scrap over the faceplate, adjusting the scrap until it matches the pattern on the wallpaper.

With the scrap lightly tacked to the faceplate, lift both off the wall and place them face down on a table. Trim the scrap to within ½ inch of the edge of the faceplate, cutting the corners. Fold the paper over and press firmly. Finally, cut the faceplate openings with a razor knife. Screw the faceplate over the opening.

HANDLING TRICKY SPOTS

Wallpapering around bulky, immovable objects or curved shapes requires some special techniques. Here's how to achieve good results.

Fixtures & pipes

To deal with a small obstruction, such as a thermostat, smooth the paper down as close to the fixture as possible, as shown at right. Razor-cut a small X

over the object, gradually enlarging the hole until the paper can be smoothed into place. Then trim any excess.

With a larger object, disassemble any parts that you can easily remove. Then smooth the strip down, letting it drape over the obstruction. Starting at one end or edge, cut the strip to the center of the object. (Since vertical slits tend to be tighter and show less than horizontal ones, use them unless a horizontal cut would be much shorter.)

Radiating out from the obstruction, cut additional little slits in the wall

■ SMALL OBJECTS

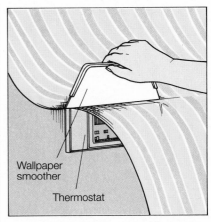

Smooth paper close to object. Then make an X-shaped cut over it, enlarging hole until paper lies flat.

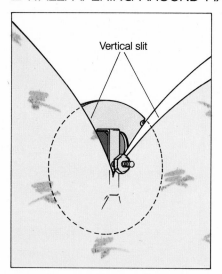

Slit wallpaper to center of fixture, cutting vertically unless side edge is much closer. Work paper all around fixture.

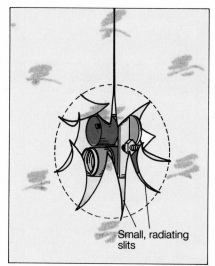

Cut numerous slits from fixture center to its outer edges until you can smooth down paper all around object.

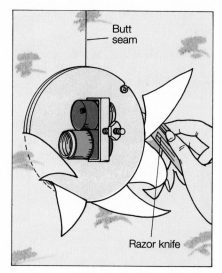

Butt edges of slit together tightly. Trim excess wallpaper around fixture with a razor knife or tuck in excess.

covering until you can smooth it all around, as shown above, center. Then finish smoothing out the strip; butt the cut edges tightly together. Trim any excess paper.

If you're papering around a sink or other fixture that doesn't abut the wall tightly, trim the paper, leaving a generous amount around the fixture, and then carefully tuck the excess behind, using a smoother or broad knife.

Curved archways

If the room you're papering has a curved archway, plan your layout carefully before you begin. You'll want to hang one strip down the center of the arch, with adjoining strips on each side, as shown below.

The amount of each side strip that hangs inside the arch should at least equal the depth of the archway.

After hanging the strips, make a horizontal cut in each side strip a few inches below where the curve of the arch begins, cutting to within 1 inch of the wall. Then wrap the lower portion of each side strip around the edge of the arch and smooth it into place. Trim the remaining paper to within 1 inch of the edge of the arch.

Using shears, make small, wedge-shaped cuts all along the unwrapped

■ WALLPAPERING CURVED ARCHWAYS

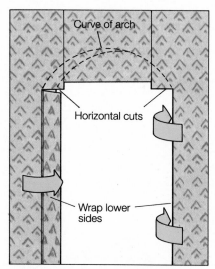

Hang strips at archway. Just below curve, cut each side strip from inner edge to within 1 inch of wall. Wrap lower sides.

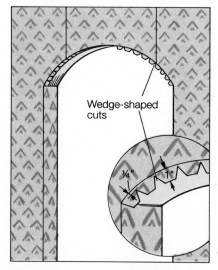

Trim remaining edges to within 1 inch of arch. Make many wedge-shaped cuts to within ¼ inch of arch. Smooth down edges.

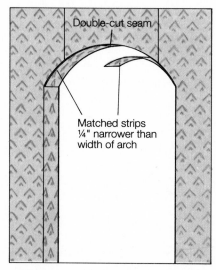

Hang matched strips from each wrapped strip to top of arch, cutting strips ¼ inch narrower than arch width to avoid fraying.

edge of the strip, cutting to within ¼ inch of the arch's edge. Carefully press the paper to the inside of the arch. (If your wallpaper is fairly thick, you may want to spackle the area between the pieces of wall covering to ensure a smooth surface; let the spackle dry before proceeding.)

To finish the underside of the arch, match and cut a strip to fit from the top of one wrapped strip to the top of the arch, and cut another strip for the other side. Make the strips ¼ inch narrower than the width of the arch to prevent fraying or peeling. Apply the strips from the side to the top, double-cutting the seam at the top.

Ceilings

In a bathroom, a small bedroom, and some other situations, extending the room's wallpaper across the ceiling can unify a decorating scheme and lend a note of drama to the room.

For best results, choose a random pattern for the walls and ceiling. This avoids having to match the pattern where the walls and ceiling meet, as well as the upside-down match you'd get along one ceiling line if you used a one-way pattern.

When planning your layout, try to run the strips across the shorter distance; this way, they'll be much more manageable. To find the square footage of the ceiling, multiply the length of the room by its width. With this figure and the information on page 75, you can determine how many rolls of wallpaper you'll need for the ceiling.

When cutting strips, allow 2 inches extra length at each end of the strips and a ½-inch overlap at each side edge. Book the strips accordion style.

To hang the paper, you'll need a ladder or, better yet, a simple scaffold created by placing a sturdy plank between two ladders. To establish plumb, first measure out from a corner of the ceiling ¼ inch less than the width of the wallpaper; mark the ceiling there. At the other corner, repeat this process. Next, tack a string rubbed with chalk to the ceiling at both these marks and snap the line, as shown at right.

You'll want to start hanging on the more noticeable side of the room or ceiling. The procedure is the same as for walls; you may want a helper to

Plumb line

Wallpaper width less ¼"

From corners, measure out width of paper minus ¼ inch. At marks, snap a plumb line.

hold the remaining length out of the way while you align the paper.

Trim the overlaps at the ceiling line to ½ inch. When you hang the walls, crease each strip at the ceiling line; cut along the crease with shears.

Caring for Wallpaper

The first step to ensuring easy maintenance and long life for your wallpaper is to choose a material that's appropriate for the room. Be especially careful in kitchens and children's rooms, where the walls will be subject to hard use. Before you buy, note carefully the pros and cons of the different wall-covering materials (see pages 73–74).

As you hang the paper, wipe off any excess adhesive from the wall covering and surrounding areas.

Protection. Applying a protective coating to a nonvinyl wallpaper lengthens its life and makes it easier to clean. Your dealer can suggest an appropriate coat-

ing for your material. Before applying it, allow the adhesive to dry thoroughly (about a week).

Wallpaper is particularly vulnerable to damage at outside corners. A plastic corner guard can prevent such problems. A wood molding strip that you can stain or paint also works well.

Cleaning. Most wallpapers come with cleaning instructions. Test any cleaning product on a scrap before using it.

To remove dirt and grime, try commercial wallpaper dough; this product will not remove stains, however. Clean stained areas on washable paper with mild soap and cold water. Then rinse

with clear, cold water and dry with a clean, absorbent cloth.

On nonwashable paper, blot, don't wash, the affected area with a sponge moistened with a solution of mild soap and cold water. Then blot with cold water and dry. For stubborn stains, have your dealer recommend a spot remover.

Repair. Press a matched, pasted scrap of the wall covering lightly against the wall over the damaged area. Make an irregularly shaped razor cut around the area through both wall coverings; lift off the patch. Remove the damaged piece as you would old wallpaper, repaste the patch, if necessary, and press it in place.

Decorating with Borders

Very popular as decorative wall accents either alone or with one or even two coordinating wallpapers, borders are especially effective along the ceiling line or at chair-rail height.

If you're hanging a border directly on a painted wall, follow the steps on pages 77–79 for preparing the surface. If you apply primer-sealer, coat just the area of the wall that the border will cover. Before installing a border over a new wall covering, let the paper dry thoroughly so the weight of the border won't pull it away from the wall.

Hanging a border is similar to hanging any wallpaper, except that most steps are easier. (For basic wallpapering instructions, see pages 80–91.) You'll have to draw your layout lines with special care, however, especially if you're combining a border with another wallpaper.

Borders at the ceiling line

If you're hanging a ceiling border over a painted wall or over wallpaper with a random match, just place the top of the border at the ceiling or molding edge. If you're hanging over paper with a straight or drop match, you'll need to check the wall height in several places to see if it varies. If it doesn't and the paper is plumb, you can simply hang the border to the ceiling or molding. If wall height does vary, you'll need layout lines.

Layout. To lay out a border, subtract its height from the shortest wall height. Then, using a carpenter's level, mark the wall all around the room at this distance from the floor, as shown below, at left. To work around an inside corner, hold the level across the corner so one end of the level touches each wall; make a mark on the new wall and then connect the lines into the corner.

Because the ceiling edge is not a true horizontal, you'll need to make adjustments as you hang. To fill in occasional gaps above the border, use some border edge scrap. Or you can wrap a bit of the border onto the ceiling. If an uneven ceiling line becomes a big problem, you may want to reconsider using a border.

Installation. Paste the entire strip with the appropriate adhesive, or, if the border is prepasted, soak it in water. If you're hanging over vinyl wallpaper, use vinyl-to-vinyl adhesive. Book the paper accordion style without creasing the folds, as shown below.

Unfold and tack up just an arm's length of paper at a time. Align the tacked section with any layout lines you drew by pushing it around with your spread fingers. Smooth the strip and wipe off excess adhesive.

If the design element at the end of the first strip matches the design at the beginning of the next one, simply butt the strips together. Otherwise, you'll have to overlap matching elements and double-cut the seam.

At inside corners, use lap seams as for wallpaper. If you want to match the pattern more exactly, join strips with double-cut seams.

Chair-rail borders

When using a border at chair-rail height, you can hang it alone, coordinate it with another wallpaper below or above, or combine it with wallpaper below and above. How you draw your layout lines and install the border paper will depend on how many papers you're hanging.

Begin by deciding at what height you want the border. For example, you may want the lower edge to align with the bottom of a window molding or with some other architectural feature.

Chair-rail border only. When you're hanging border paper alone, use a level

■ HANGING A CEILING BORDER OVER WALLPAPER

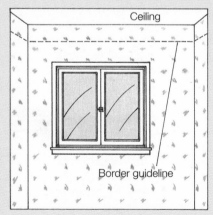

If border is going over paper with a straight or drop match and wall height varies slightly, draw a layout line all around room.

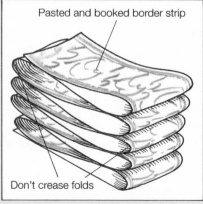

Paste or soak border strip. Book pasted strip using an accordion-style fold, pasted sides together; avoid creasing paper.

Align first part of border with guideline; then smooth that section to wall. Install an arm's length of paper at a time.

■ CHAIR-RAIL BORDER WITH WALLPAPER BELOW

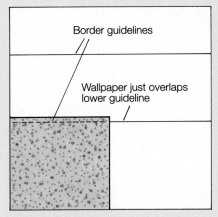

Border guidelines

Wallpaper just overlaps lower guideline

Using a carpenter's level, draw guidelines for top and bottom edges of border. Hang wallpaper so it just overlaps lower line.

Hang border to upper guideline

Metal straightedge

Razor knife

Hang border, aligning its top edge with upper guideline. Cut along bottom edge of border. Lift to remove scrap underneath.

to mark all around the room where you want the top or bottom edge to lie, using the same technique as for ceiling borders. Hang the paper, aligning the edge with the line you drew on the wall.

Chair-rail border with wallpaper below or above. Using a carpenter's level, draw layout lines for the top and bottom edges of the border, as shown above.

For wallpaper below a border, hang the paper across the first wall, allowing it to slightly overlap the lower guideline. Then, using the upper line as a guide, hang the border. Holding a straightedge or broad knife at the bottom edge of the

border, cut the excess paper underneath the border. Lift up the lower edge of the border and remove the excess paper underneath. Smooth down the border and roll the seam. Complete the room one wall at a time.

For wallpaper going above the border, hang it so it overlaps the upper guideline; continue as appropriate.

Chair-rail border with wallpaper below and above. Use a level to draw a horizontal line on the wall at about the middle of the border area. (Be sure to consider the vertical placement of the papers above and below so the border doesn't cut designs inappropriately.)

Install a strip of the top paper; then, guiding the razor knife with a straightedge, trim the paper to the line, as shown below, at left. (You'll be able to see the line on either side of the strip.) Continue all around the room until you've hung all of the first paper.

Next, hang the bottom strips, butting or double-cutting the ends where they meet the wallpaper above. Finally, hang the border, aligning it with a design element on the wallpaper or with a new line drawn on the wallpaper.

Borders around doors & windows

When two border strips intersect from different angles, you can achieve pattern continuity by matching the design and then making a mitered cut, as shown below. This technique works best with nondirectional papers.

On the pasting table, arrange the two strips so the pattern matches and the pieces completely overlap in the corner. (With some patterns, you may want to line up a specific design element over the center of the opening.) Install the first strip.

Hang the second strip lightly, matching the pattern again. Double-cut diagonally through both strips with a razor knife and carpenter's triangle. Carefully remove the scrap pieces on top and underneath; then roll the seam.

■ CHAIR-RAIL BORDER WITH TWO WALLPAPERS

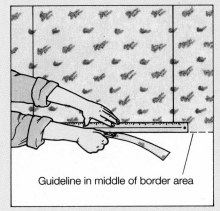

Guideline in middle of border area

Draw a line at about middle of border area and hang upper paper to just below line. Trim paper flush with line.

Align border with design element in wallpaper

Butt or double-cut second paper where it meets first. Hang border, aligning it with design in wallpaper or with a new line.

■ MITERING BORDER STRIPS

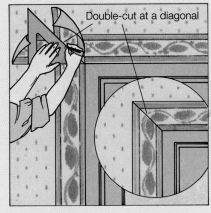

Double-cut at a diagonal

Hang intersecting border strips so pattern matches; double-cut corner diagonally. Lift to remove scrap underneath.

Fabric

Something special happens when you cover your walls with fabric. Whether it's crisp chintz, informal canvas, or shimmering moiré, fabric makes walls come alive with color, pattern, and texture. Like no other wall covering, fabric lends softness and warmth to a room. Best of all, you don't have to be an expert to achieve professional results. All you need are accurate measurements, a steady hand, and patience.   Even if you decide to apply fabric to your walls just because you love the look, you'll soon discover that each method has its own characteristics to consider. Walls upholstered with fabric over batting lend quiet elegance to any setting; the batting provides insulating and acoustic benefits as well. Stapling fabric to walls is a quick and easy way to transform a room, and pasted walls are perfect if you don't sew.   Moreover, because fabric walls make such a strong statement, fabric allows you to express your individuality and creativity. Think of the fabric as an important design element, dressing up walls and tying together an assortment of furnishings and accessories.   For inspiration, look through the colorful examples on these pages. Then turn to the how-to section for an overview of each technique, guidelines for choosing fabric, and step-by-step instructions that will lead you from beginning to end of each installation.

Spirited hues and a lively mix of patterns typify French country cottons. For color continuity, the upholstered walls wear the same fabric as the window and bed canopy. Companion borders and prints complete the coordinated look. Design: Pierre Deux Original Fabrics.

LUXURIOUS UPHOLSTERED WALLS

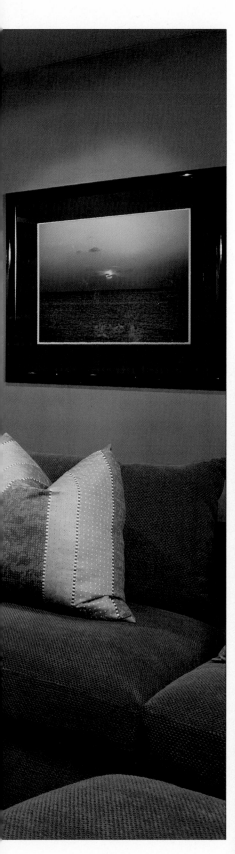

Walls upholstered in cocoa-colored synthetic suede soften this contemporary room and provide a striking backdrop for art. The oversized pillows and sofa echo the plushness of the walls. Interior design: Janice M. Stein of Villa Associates. Upholstered walls: Douglas Griggs of Hang Ups.

Double welt does double duty outlining a graceful curve and concealing the staples and raw edges of the fabric underneath (for a larger view of the wall, see below). Cut-on-the-bias casings allow the welt to bend smoothly when it's applied to the wall.

Sumptuous moiré meets glowing mahogany in this elegant neoclassical design. The icy blue upholstered walls, as rich looking as the woodwork that surrounds them, complement the botanical drawings in their Federal-style frames. Interior design: Tedrick & Bennett. Upholstered walls: Douglas Griggs of Hang Ups.

FABRIC BACKGROUNDS: FANCIFUL TO FORMAL

Playful circus characters decorate a canvas wall hanging in this child's room. Because it's painted on fabric rather than on the wall, this mural can be moved easily. The solo trapeze artist can come down anytime, too—he's painted on canvas and then cut out and lightly glued to the wall. Decorative artist: Ann Blair Davison.

For an understated look, the best color is sometimes a noncolor. Walls upholstered in straightforward off-white cotton keep the focus on the furnishings and art; a simple wallpaper border at the top unifies the neutral walls and contrasting molding. Upholstered walls: Tony Vella.

Warm wood and cognac-colored moiré upholstered walls extend a formal welcome in this handsome entry. The striped walls and mahogany paneling establish strong vertical lines; the balloon shade introduces contrasting curves. Interior design: John Tobler

Fabric: Your Choices

As popular in today's contemporary homes as in the formal palaces of the past, fabric walls lend vitality, texture, and color to a room. Three techniques for applying fabric to walls—upholstering, stapling, and pasting—are described here; for detailed installation instructions, see pages 101–107. Also presented here are suggestions for selecting the right fabric for your walls.

Three fabric techniques

To decide which technique is best for you, think about the look you want to achieve and the amount of time and effort you're willing to spend on the project. With all three fabric-application methods, you can remove the fabric when you get tired of it and reuse it for pillows, curtains, or other projects.

Upholstered walls. Covering walls with fabric and batting takes more time than stapling or pasting fabric on walls, but once you're finished, you'll agree that upholstered walls are worth the work. Batting under the fabric cushions the walls, provides soundproofing and insulation, and gives the fabric a soft, luxurious appearance. Trim, usually double welt, is used to finish the edges.

Upholstered walls successfully conceal almost all wall imperfections, such as cracks and uneven surfaces.

The most suitable rooms for wall upholstery are those that don't receive heavy use—bedrooms, dining rooms, and living rooms. Upholstered walls are not recommended for kitchens and bathrooms, where grease and steam are problems.

You can upholster the ceiling as well, but it's best to do so only in a small room because you'll have to stretch the fabric tightly and anchor it in several places to prevent sagging.

Test the wall to see if stapling will damage it. Generally, the small holes left by the staples can be filled with paint or a coat of spackle if you decide to remove the fabric later. If the staples can't puncture the surface, or if they leave large holes and chip the wall, you can mount furring strips as for wood paneling (see page 119) to provide a good working surface.

Stapled walls. For this simple application, you stitch together panels of fabric in the same way as for upholstered walls and install the fabric covers similarly. But with stapled walls, you don't have to work over batting or place the staples quite so close together. Also, you use an easy technique around corners.

If you want to simulate the appearance of upholstered walls and significantly increase the insulating and acoustic qualities of the wall, choose a quilted fabric.

Pasted walls. Pasting fabric on walls differs from most other wall-covering techniques in that you apply adhesive to the wall, not to the wall covering. Fabric pasted on walls is resistant to steam and can be easily removed without causing damage to the wall; any paste residue left on the walls can be washed off.

But before you decide to paste fabric on your walls, consider the following drawbacks: This application reveals any bumps, cracks, or other wall damage, so walls must be perfectly smooth. Also, colored walls must be given a coat of primer so light-colored fabrics won't appear tinted.

Guidelines for choosing fabric

When it comes to fabric, the options are endless. Deciding on just one may seem as challenging as the work of putting it up on the wall.

Before you commit to yards and yards of a certain fabric, consider both its appearance and its suitability for the application you have in mind. All three techniques require approximately the same amount of fabric; for upholstered walls, you'll also need batting.

Here are some suggestions to help you shop for fabric.

■ Home decorating and upholstery fabrics are excellent choices. Look for them in fabric stores, home furnishings fabric shops, and upholstery shops. Available in widths up to 60 inches, these fabrics are usually treated with a repellent that inhibits stains and dust collection. In addition, they're printed with pattern overlaps at the selvages, making it easy to match the pattern at the seams.

■ If you're upholstering or stapling, you can also consider flat bed sheets. (Their size makes them hard to handle if you're pasting.) Less expensive than home decorating or upholstery fabrics, sheets come in an enormous variety of colors and designs. To determine the size and number you'll need, use these flat sheet finished dimensions: twin, 66 by 96 inches; double, 81 by 96 inches; queen, 90 by 102 inches; and king, 108 by 102 inches.

■ Be cautious when selecting a printed fabric. Usually the print will be slightly off-grain—veering at an angle from the lengthwise and crosswise threads. Often, the misalignment isn't noticeable. But if it is, don't use the fabric, since it won't hang properly.

To check the fabric, fold it back a few inches along the horizontal grain, wrong sides together, aligning selvages. If the print runs evenly along the fold, it's fairly well aligned. If the print wanders across the fold, it's badly off-grain.

■ If you're pasting, note the fabric recommendations on page 107.

■ Fabrics with allover designs are the easiest to work with because the pattern can help camouflage wall imperfections and uneven ceiling lines. They also show less soil than those with large, open-ground patterns.

■ Avoid stripes, plaids, and large geometric patterns for your first project, since any mistakes in application will be distractingly obvious.

■ Buy a yard or two of fabric to try out at home; pin it to the wall. After a few days, you'll know if it's right for you.

Upholstering Walls

To upholster a wall, you begin by stapling batting to the wall. Then you staple fabric covers—panels of fabric seamed together—to the wall over the batting; you'll need a separate cover for each wall you're upholstering. Finally, you cover the staples and fabric edges with double welt or another trim.

If you want to upholster the ceiling as well, do it before the walls.

BASIC EQUIPMENT

The most important piece of equipment you'll need is a staple gun, along with a full box of ⅜-inch staples. An electric staple gun, available from a tool rental company, will speed your work and prevent aching arms and fingers, but because most electric guns have their motors at the head, you can't use them along the ceiling line (unless there's a ceiling molding) or in corners. For this close work, you'll need a hand-held staple gun.

A tack hammer may come in handy for tapping in any staples that don't penetrate deeply enough. You'll need cardboard tack strips to hold the stapled fabric securely and maintain sharp edges in corners. You can purchase strips in an upholstery shop; buy enough stripping to run the height of the wall for all inside corners to be covered, except the corner where you begin and end (no strip is used there).

A steel tape measure, more accurate than a fabric tape, is an essential tool. Use an electric glue gun and hot-melt glue to attach trim to fabric edges, and fabric glue or spray adhesive to cover faceplates with fabric.

Also have a staple remover, fabric shears, long push pins (the ¾-inch size

*For **upholstering walls,** helpful tools include (1) tack hammer, (2) electric staple gun, (3) steel tape measure, (4) hand-held staple gun, (5) broad knife, (6) hot-melt glue sticks, (7) razor or utility knife, (8) tack strips, (9) electric glue gun.*

available in stationery stores), a razor knife (preferably the type with snap-off blades) or a utility knife, a supply of extra blades, a broad knife or metal straightedge, and a screwdriver.

When you staple along the ceiling line or below any molding, use a sturdy ladder. A sewing machine is essential for stitching together lengths of fabric to make the separate covers. Use an iron to remove fabric creases and to press the seams open.

DETERMINING YARDAGE

Before you make your purchases, take time to check and recheck the total yardage figures required for each material. These figures include a margin

of safety that will ensure you'll have enough material to complete the project. It's always possible that the same pattern or dye lot won't be available later if you need more material.

Measuring for fabric

Use a long steel tape measure to make your measurements. Mark the dimensions on paper—you'll need to use the figures to make the yardage calculations and to determine cutting lines. As you measure, keep in mind that each wall is to be covered with a separate fabric cover.

Width measurement. Separately measure the width (in inches) of each wall you're planning to cover, unless you'll be working around an outside corner; in that case you'll use one fabric cover, starting it at one wall edge, wrapping it around the corner, and continuing to the far edge of the wall.

To find the number of fabric panels required for one wall, divide the

■ UPHOLSTERY EQUIPMENT

width of the wall by the usable width of the fabric, taking into account the amount of fabric taken up in seams (allow ½-inch seam allowances).

If your calculations result in a fraction, round up to the next whole number of fabric panels. This extra fabric width will give you some leeway to match the pattern at corners.

Height measurement. Measure the height (in inches) of the same wall from the ceiling line (or lower edge of the ceiling molding) to the top of the baseboard. Take this measurement in several places to check for variations; use the largest figure.

Add 6 inches to the height measurement as insurance against errors. If the fabric has a pattern repeat, add the repeat length to the height measurement to allow for matching the pattern at the seams. Your final figure is the working height of the wall.

Total fabric yardage. Multiply the working height figure by the number of fabric panels needed for the wall; divide this figure by 36 to convert to the number of running yards of fabric required for the wall you've measured.

Repeat the calculations for each wall you're covering. Add together the running yards for all the walls to determine total fabric yardage. Add extra yardage if you plan to finish the walls with double welt (instructions for measuring for trim appear at right).

Determining batting yardage

To pad the walls, use ¾-inch bonded polyester batting. Available 48, 54, or 96 inches wide, batting can be purchased in large fabric stores or in home furnishings or upholstery fabric shops.

To compute the amount of batting you'll need, measure (in inches) the exact height and width of the area to be covered; *do not* add extra inches.

Total the width measurements of the walls and divide by the width of the batting to determine how many strips of batting you need; round up to the next whole number. Multiply this figure by the height of the wall and convert to yards to compute how much batting is required.

Dimensions of large openings, such as sliding doors and picture windows, can be subtracted from your yardage figure, since batting can be pieced around openings.

Measuring for trim

Double welt made of the same fabric as that on the wall or of a complementary fabric is the traditional finish. (To make double welt, see page 106.) Or you can use heavy grosgrain ribbon (glue will show through lightweight ribbon), braid, or gimp in the same color or, for a different effect, in a contrasting color. Molding that's stained, painted, or wrapped with fabric also makes an attractive trim.

Plan to use a continuous strip of trim (unless you're using molding) for the perimeter of the area to be covered. To determine how much trim you'll need, track in your mind a course that starts at an inconspicuous corner, as shown at right, travels around the upholstered area at floor level, goes up the wall at the starting corner, and tracks around the top edge.

Measure this distance and round up to the next half-yard figure to provide a margin of safety. Also measure around the edges of all unconnected openings, such as windows, that must be trimmed. Add all measurements together to determine the total yardage.

PREPARING FABRIC & BATTING

If the fabric has an allover print, it's not necessary to plan where the seams will hang on the wall; once the fabric is stretched over the wall, the seams won't show. But if you're using a solid-color fabric, seams will be noticeable, so you'll want to plan their placement where they'll be the least conspicuous. If the fabric has predominant motifs, you may want to center the pattern on the first wall.

Cutting the fabric. Spread the fabric out on a flat, smooth surface. Using tailor's chalk or a pencil, mark the point on the pattern that will lie along the ceiling line. From that point down, mea-

■ MEASURING FOR TRIM

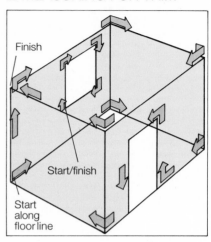

Starting at a corner, measure room along floor, moving around doors. At starting point, measure up corner of wall and along top edge. Measure windows separately.

sure and mark the length of the first strip according to the height measurement you recorded.

Cut the fabric at the top and bottom markings. Continue cutting fabric panels, matching any pattern, until you have enough to cover one wall. Make sure the panels run in the same direction—reversing the nap can produce color variation that may be apparent only after the fabric is on the wall.

If you're using a light-colored fabric with printing on the selvages, such as the manufacturer's name or color keys, cut them off.

To avoid confusion, pin together the panels you've just cut for the first fabric cover before continuing. Be sure the pattern placement at the top is the same for all subsequent fabric panels you cut.

Stitching the seams. Pin the fabric panels, right sides together; be sure to match any pattern. Using ½-inch seam allowances and starting at the top edge, stitch the panels; backstitch at the beginning and end of each seam. If you haven't trimmed the selvages, clip them every few inches so the seam allowances will lie flat. Press the seams open and press out any creases.

Cutting the batting. Measure strips of batting in lengths equal to the height of the wall. Cut enough strips to cover the entire area you're upholstering; you'll fit the batting for width when you staple it to the walls.

APPLYING BATTING, FABRIC & TRIM

Plan to work from left to right around the room (unless you're left-handed, in which case you may find it more comfortable to work from right to left).

You'll need to remove everything from the surfaces that you're planning to upholster. Before unscrewing any faceplates, turn off the power to the room to prevent accidents when you're working around electrical openings.

Remember that if you're upholstering the ceiling, you need to do that work before you cover the walls.

Hanging batting

It's best to start in the least conspicuous corner or at the edge of an opening that runs from floor to ceiling.

Position the first strip of batting ¾ inch away from the edges of the wall and ceiling (or molding). You'll use that space to staple the fabric cover to the wall. If batting is caught in the staples holding the fabric, the staples will cause dents or ridges to appear when the fabric is stretched across the wall.

Placing the staples at least an inch in from the edge of the batting and about a foot apart, staple the batting strips along the top. (Don't staple along the edge of the batting, or dents will appear.) Staple down the left side and then down the right side of the batting. Cut any excess off the bottom edge, leaving a ¾-inch space between the batting and the baseboard; staple across the bottom.

Butt the second batting strip against the first and staple it in the same way, as shown in Step 1 on page 104. Continue until the entire area is covered. At inside corners, stop the batting ¾ inch from the corner; wrap batting around outside corners as for wallpaper (see page 87).

Cut the batting ¾ inch away from the edges of all openings, except receptacles and switches. Since these will be covered with faceplates, carefully trim the batting just to the opening's edge.

Applying fabric covers

Refer to the illustrations on page 104 as you staple the fabric covers over the batting.

Stapling the first wall. If you're centering a large motif on the first wall, measure the distance from the center of the wall to the left corner and then measure the same distance on the fabric cover from the center of the motif to the left. Cut the fabric cover lengthwise at that point, being careful to cut exactly on the lengthwise grain.

Position the fabric cover so the left side hangs down the edge of the wall and the top edge of the fabric is aligned with the ceiling line or molding. Holding the fabric along the top and working from left to right, use push pins to pin the fabric in place along the top edge for 3 to 4 feet; let the remaining fabric hang freely.

Starting at the top corner and working down, staple the left side of the fabric to the wall, positioning the staples parallel to the wall edge (see Step 2) and about the width of a staple apart from each other. (The staples must be close together so the fabric won't ripple when it's pulled taut.)

Return to the top edge and staple the fabric that's being held with push pins. Then, holding the remaining fabric in your right hand, extend your arm to the right as far as you can reach; staple the fabric in place at that point.

Staple the top edge of the fabric from left to right, as shown in Step 3, until you reach the far staple. Repeat the procedure to the end of the wall. When working around an outside corner, continue stapling as described, pulling the fabric tightly around the corner.

With the left side and top edge of the fabric cover in place, check that the seams are straight. Hang a plumb line down the seam that's farthest right as for wallpaper (see page 81). Straighten the seam by pulling the fabric taut at the bottom edge; staple the lower edge of the fabric at the seamline to hold it in place.

Check the seams to the left—they should be straight. Staple the lower edge of each seam in place.

If you're upholstering only one wall and you're not working around any inside corners, you're ready to staple along the bottom edge (instructions follow). But if you're upholstering walls with inside corners, follow the directions below.

Stapling an inside corner. Stretch the fabric around the inside corner. Using staple gun pressure and your hand to pull the fabric taut to the second wall, staple the fabric to the second wall from top to bottom as far into the corner as possible (see Step 4), placing staples parallel to the corner edge; be sure not to catch batting in the staples.

Using push pins, tack the fabric cover for the second wall along the top edge of the first wall, right sides together. To match any pattern, align the edge of the second fabric cover to the pattern of the first one. Use the vertical line in the pattern or the fabric grainline to ensure that the pattern is matched all the way down the wall.

Staple the second fabric cover at several points in the corner down the second wall (see Step 5); as you staple, remove the push pins and flip the fabric over to check pattern alignment. Remove staples and make adjustments, if necessary. Trim any excess fabric from the corner.

Push a tack strip tightly into the corner on the second wall. Staple the tack strip to the wall over both fabric layers, as shown in Step 6; the strip will hold the fabric tightly in place and make a smooth, flat corner edge.

Butt a second tack strip to the bottom of the first and staple it in place. Apply additional strips, if necessary, in the same manner; use shears to trim the bottom strip to fit. Remove the push pins, bring the second fabric cover over to the second wall, and pin it 3 to 4 feet along the top edge.

Stapling the bottom edge. Staple the bottom edge of the first fabric cover, keeping staples as close to the baseboard as possible.

Protecting the fabric cover with a broad knife or metal straightedge, use

1 Positioning batting ¾ inch away from wall and ceiling edges, staple strips to wall, butting adjacent strips. Place staples about a foot apart.

2 With push pins, pin fabric along ceiling line or molding edge for 3 to 4 feet. Starting at top, staple left side of fabric, taking care not to catch batting in staples.

3 After stapling fabric being held with pins, gently pull fabric taut along top edge and staple as far as you can reach; then staple from left to right close to edge.

4 At inside corner, stretch fabric around corner. Using your hand and staple gun pressure to pull fabric taut, staple fabric to second wall as far into corner as possible.

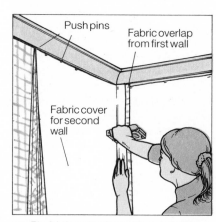

5 Pin fabric cover for second wall over first wall, right sides together. Carefully matching pattern down wall, staple second cover into corner at 1-foot intervals.

6 After trimming any excess fabric, push a tack strip into corner against second wall. Staple strip in place over both fabric layers, using a hand-held staple gun.

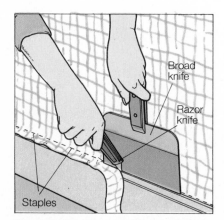

7 Staple fabric to wall along top of baseboard. Using a broad knife to protect fabric, carefully trim excess fabric with a razor knife.

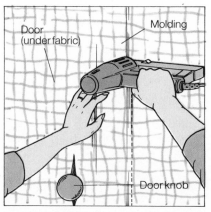

8 Staple close to molding around a door or other opening. Carefully cut fabric at door knob and corners of molding to allow fabric to lie flat.

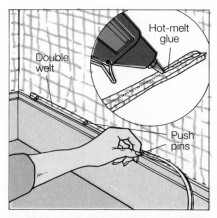

9 Using an electric glue gun, apply hot-melt glue to underside of welt (see inset). Tack welt in place with push pins; remove pins when glue has dried.

a razor knife to cut excess fabric along the top of the baseboard (see Step 7). Keep the razor blade flat against the wall; change blades frequently to avoid pulled and stretched fabric edges. If you're covering only one wall, finish the edge as you would the last wall edge (see directions below).

Stapling the second wall. Extend the second fabric cover to the right as far as you can reach; staple it in place along the top. Continue stapling, following the procedure for the first fabric cover. Taking care to match any pattern and form sharp corners, attach the remaining fabric covers in the same manner.

Finishing the last wall edge. How you staple the last side of the fabric cover depends on the type of wall edge you've reached.

If you've worked around the room and have returned to the first wall, staple the last side to the first wall over the staples where you began. Carefully cut excess fabric away with fabric shears. Later, you'll glue trim over these staples to finish the edge.

If the final fabric side is along the edge of a floor-to-ceiling opening or in a corner, staple the fabric close to the edge of the wall. Trim excess fabric with a razor knife.

Covering narrow spaces. A strip of wall that's less than 4 inches wide is very difficult to upholster using the method just described. Instead, cut a piece of poster board to fit the space. Using no batting, wrap the fabric around the poster board and glue the edges in place on the back. Using brads, tack the covered strip to the wall; poke the nail heads under the fabric.

Working around openings. To expose doors and windows that have been hidden under the fabric, follow these directions.

Starting at the bottom edge of the molding, staple the fabric to the wall as close to the molding as possible (see Step 8); don't catch batting in the staples. As you staple, cut holes for door knobs and molding corners to pop through so you can keep the fabric taut across the wall surface. When stapling is com-

pleted, use a razor knife to cut the fabric along the molding edge, protecting the fabric with a broad knife.

Covering faceplates. You can cover faceplates with fabric to match the wall. Use fabric glue for this job; spray contact cement can also be used, but it dries in a yellow color, so it's not satisfactory for light-colored fabrics. Before beginning work, be sure the electricity is turned off.

Find the opening by feel and carefully cut the fabric along the edges of the opening. Spread glue on the front of the faceplate and position it over the opening. Place a scrap of fabric over it, matching the pattern of the fabric to the pattern on the wall.

Remove the faceplate and smooth the fabric on the front. Trim within ½ inch of the edge, cut away the corners, and glue, as shown at right. Razor-cut along the edges of the openings on the faceplate and punch holes at the screw openings. Trim any loose threads.

Finishing with trim

Applying trim is the easiest part of installing a fabric wall. Double welt, grosgrain ribbon, braid, gimp, and molding all provide a professional-looking finish to your project.

Double welt. Make one continuous strip of double welt (see page 106). If you're upholstering the entire room, you'll apply welt around the baseboard, up the corner where you began, and finally around the top edge, using separate strips for each.

Using an electric glue gun, apply a 12-inch-long strip of hot-melt glue to the underside (the side with the raw edge) of the welt along the center stitching line, as shown in Step 9 (see inset). Place the welt along the bottom edge of the fabric cover a few inches from the corner; face the raw edge toward the baseboard. Tack the trim with push pins. Repeat the procedure for the next section of welt.

To work around corners, press the welt firmly and tightly into place with a screwdriver. Long push pins come in handy here to hold the welt securely until the glue dries.

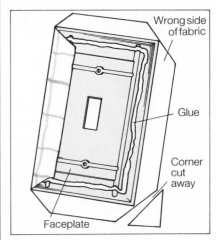

Cut off corners of fabric, apply a thin strip of glue to wrong side of faceplate, and wrap fabric around plate, pressing tightly.

To finish the ends along the baseboard or top edge, cut the welt so it's an inch longer than the area remaining to be covered. Push the welt fabric back to expose both cords; cut an inch off the end of each cord. Fold the welt fabric ½ inch to the wrong side; spread with fabric glue. Apply the remaining welt to the wall, letting the cordless fabric overlap the end of the welt.

Ribbon, braid, or gimp. Apply these trims in the same manner as double welt. If you're using hot-melt glue to attach grosgrain ribbon, work quickly, or the glue will harden and leave a visible ridge. If the braid is too bulky to turn under, cut the edge so it butts against the first braid end. Use fabric glue to keep the edges from fraying.

Molding. Molding can be stained, painted, or covered with fabric. To cover with fabric, simply wrap a strip of fabric around the molding; glue the edges in place on the wrong side. Using brads, tack the molding to the wall at the edge of the fabric cover.

Fabric care

To prevent stains, treat the walls with a stain repellent. On all fabric walls, you can spray the fabric after installation; be sure to follow the manufacturer's instructions. For normal cleaning, simply vacuum the walls.

Stapling Fabric to Walls

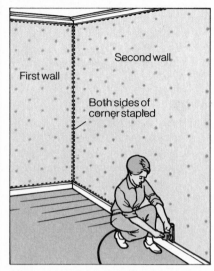

Stapling is the simplest, fastest way to add color and design to plain walls.

Tools & supplies

A staple gun is a must, as is a large box of ⅜-inch staples (½-inch staples for quilted fabrics). Also have on hand a steel tape measure, fabric shears, a razor knife with snap-off blades, a broad knife or metal straightedge, a staple remover, and a ladder.

If you'll be stitching panels of fabric together, you'll want a sewing machine and an iron.

Stapling from start to finish

If you need to use furring strips, install them as you would for paneling; see the directions on page 119. Measure and prepare the fabric covers following the instructions on pages 101–102.

To staple the covers to the wall, follow the same progression as for upholstered walls (see pages 103–105): left side, top edge, right side, and bottom. Place the staples 2 to 3 inches apart.

Corners of stapled walls are easy to handle. Simply stretch the fabric for the first wall to the corner and staple it to the first wall as far into the corner as possible. Protecting the fabric with a broad knife, use a razor knife to trim excess fabric.

Start the second wall fabric cover in the same manner as the first wall, matching the pattern as closely as possible. Staple all edges (see at right). To work around openings, see page 105.

Cover the staples and raw edges with trim when all walls are stapled. To determine trim length, see page 102, but remember to add twice the wall height measurement to your total for

Staple fabric into both sides of corners and along ceiling (or molding) and baseboard, placing staples 2 to 3 inches apart.

each corner (you need to cover the raw edges and staples on both sides of every corner). Instructions for applying the trim and for caring for the fabric appear on page 105.

How to Make Double Welt

Double welt is the professionals' choice to cover fabric edges and staples decoratively.

Gathering materials. To measure the amount of welt you'll need, see the section on measuring for trim on page 102. Purchase ¼-inch cord twice the length of the trim measurement. Make the casing for the cord from fabric strips cut on the bias. You'll need enough 1¾-inch-wide bias strips to make a welt equal to the trim measurement.

Use the following guidelines for purchasing fabric: If your fabric is 45 inches wide, buy 1 yard of fabric for every 23 yards of welt you're making. For 54-inch-wide fabric, you'll need 1 yard of fabric for every 28 yards of welt.

You'll also need a sewing machine equipped with a zipper foot, a tape measure, and a straightedge.

Stitching welt. Cut enough bias strips to make a continuous welt and stitch the strips together, using a ¼-inch seam allowance.

Begin by wrapping one edge of the casing around a piece of cord, leaving a ⅛- to ¼-inch flap of fabric (see at right). Using the zipper foot, stitch close to the cord the entire length of the casing.

Place the second piece of cord on the wrong side of the fabric next to the stitching line. Wrap the fabric over the cord. Then turn the welt to the front. Using the regular presser foot, stitch over the first stitching line; hold the fab-

ric securely so the cords stay close together and are tightly bound.

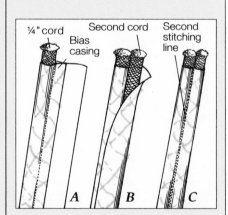

Wrap casing around cord and stitch (A). Fold fabric over second cord (B); turn to front and stitch again (C).

Pasting Fabric on Walls

To paste fabric on walls, you simply apply adhesive to each wall, a small section at a time, and then smooth down fabric panels. Note, however, that this application is recommended only for very smooth, light-colored walls. (To prepare your walls, see pages 38–40.)

Be sure to choose your fabric carefully. Light-colored fabrics with allover patterns work best. Fabrics with nap or porosity, such as velvet and wool, are not suitable for pasting. Nor are dark-colored fabrics—adhesive can stain the fabric, and dark fabric dyes can bleed onto the wall.

Border fabric can be pasted on top of fabric walls as a trim after the walls are completely dry. Use the procedure for pasting panels described below right, being careful not to drip adhesive onto the fabric.

If you decide to remove the fabric later on, start from a corner along the baseboard and gently peel the fabric from the wall. The adhesive will come off with the fabric without damaging the wall surface. Using a damp sponge, wash the wall to remove any residue.

Helpful tools & supplies

Essential are a plumb line, a paint roller, a razor knife with snap-off blades, and a broad knife or metal straightedge.

You'll also need vinyl wallpaper adhesive, a large sponge, a paint tray for the adhesive, and several drop cloths to cover the floor. Fabric shears and some ¾-inch push pins complete the list of supplies.

Before you paste

Measure the area to be covered and determine the amount of fabric you'll need, following the directions for wallpaper (see page 75). When calculating the usable width of the fabric, deduct the selvages that must be trimmed before the panels are joined on the wall.

It's best to join panels using butted edges—you can match the pattern more easily, and, with fabric, the seams won't shrink away when they dry.

Measure and cut the panels according to the directions on pages 101–102, with two differences: instead of adding 6 inches to the length for insurance, cut the top edge of the fabric 2 inches above where you want the pattern to appear along the ceiling line or molding; also, cut the bottom edge of the panel 2 inches below the baseboard.

Working on a hard, flat surface, cut the selvages from the fabric, using a razor knife with a sharp blade and holding a broad knife or metal straightedge against the fabric to prevent any razor mishaps.

Clean the walls thoroughly and let them dry. If the walls are a dark color, apply a primer (see page 35). Put a small amount of adhesive in the paint tray; add enough water to thin the adhesive to the consistency of cream soup.

Pasting the panels

Establish plumb as for wallpaper (see page 81) and align the pattern along the top edge; remember to leave a 2-inch overlap. Tack the fabric along the top with push pins. Check to be sure the fabric is even with the plumb line; if it's not, adjust the fabric.

Lift the fabric out of the way and tack it to one side. Using a paint roller or brush, apply adhesive to the wall, starting at the top edge and pasting down a few feet, as shown in the drawing at right; cover an area a few inches wider than the width of the fabric.

Remove the pins from the side-draped fabric but not from the top edge. With your hands, lightly smooth the fabric into place, working from the center out to the sides and being careful not to stretch the fabric. Make sure the edges are firmly in place. Paste down any loose threads or cut them off; don't try to pull the threads.

To eliminate bubbles, brush a little adhesive on the front of the fabric until it lies flat. To eliminate wrinkles, brush adhesive on the fabric and use your fingernail to smooth them out. Be sure to wipe off the surface with a damp sponge before the adhesive dries.

Tack the remaining fabric to the side and apply adhesive a few more feet down the wall. Repeat until the panel is completely pasted. Wipe any excess adhesive from the surface with a damp sponge. Moisten the fabric overlaps at the top and baseboard edges with adhesive. When dry, they'll be easy to cut off with a razor knife.

Paste the remaining fabric panels. To work around corners, openings, and fixtures, use the same techniques as for wallpaper (see pages 86–90).

If you must leave your project overnight, place the adhesive and brushes in plastic bags and store them in the refrigerator until the next day.

When the fabric has dried (at least 24 hours), use a razor knife to trim the overlapping fabric along the top and the baseboard; protect the fabric with a broad knife or metal straightedge.

If the razor edge slips while you're cutting, repaste the area and pat a matching fabric patch in place. When the adhesive dries, cut off any loose threads and the patch won't be visible. You can also use this technique later, in the event of stains or damage.

■ APPLYING ADHESIVE

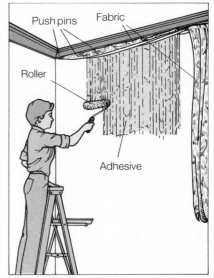

With fabric tacked at ceiling line and off to side, apply adhesive to wall one section at a time.

Paneling

THE WARMTH OF WOOD

Picture sitting by the fire on a quiet evening, curling up in a cozy study with a good book, or gathering friends together for a holiday dinner party, and you'll probably envision the texture and warmth of a paneled room. Wood paneling, whether made of solid boards or sheets, adapts to any setting. You can choose from among many species, each with its own character. Some are perfect for casual, rugged appearances; others can enhance the elegance of formal rooms.   Moldings, on the wane in recent years, are enjoying yet another renaissance. Use them to evoke a period decor, to add architectural weight and drama, or simply to provide a subtle accent to new or existing wall coverings.   This chapter begins with colorful examples of the various types of wood paneling and molding. Descriptions of each type, along with instructions on how to prepare walls, how to install sheet and board paneling, and how to apply moldings, follow.   No matter what installation you choose, you'll find that with some simple carpentry tools and skills, you can transform an existing room into an exciting new environment.

Wall panels and moldings were originally painted a dark brownish green. The wood was stripped of its paint, bleached three times, and then lightly pickled to match the adjacent limestone fireplace. Nestled in the picture rail is built-in accent lighting. Interior design: Suzanne Tucker McMicking. Restoration: Steve Anderson of Wood Think It Was New.

A SOLID-BOARD LINEUP

The random-width pine paneling along one wall of this living room was already in place; the new furnishings blend right in. Ceiling beams and built-in shelving complement the beaded paneling boards. All pine surfaces were darkened with a semitransparent wiping stain. Interior design: Teresa Quigley of Spending Wives Designs.

Clear All Heart redwood teams up with Chinese slate and glass block in this bathroom design. The walls are lined with tongue-and-groove 1 by 6s; the ceiling and soffits are paneled to match. All wood surfaces are sealed with a mat varnish. Architects: Andy Neumann and Scott Rowland of Seaside Union Architects.

Ponderosa pine paneling and matching moldings dress up a peaked garage-top room. Each knotty 1 by 4 is beaded down the center to look like two boards; the wood is finished with a light wiping stain to offset yellowing. Design: Czopek & Erdenberger.

Beaded wainscoting adds a clean white accent below subtly patterned wallpaper. The narrow-looking boards are actually tongue-and-groove 1 by 6s capped by a traditional chair rail. Baseboard detailing completes the assembly. Note the smooth transition from chair rail to countertop. Architect: Remick Associates.

SHEET PRODUCTS: PLAIN & FANCY

A formal library calls for formal paneling, and these classic frame-and-panel blocks fill the order. The units are assembled from ½-inch mahogany plywood panels surrounded by built-up solid-lumber rails and stiles; crown and base molding combinations finish off the top and bottom. A red mahogany stain and hand-rubbed finish coat provide rich color and luster. You can also purchase preassembled "library panels" from some manufacturers and add your own trim. Design: Branagh Development.

Traditional wall treatment mixing bands of smooth wood with sets of vertical beads only looks complicated. Actually, it's easy-to-install hardwood plywood. The 4-by 8-foot sheets are ¼ inch thick and are simply glued or nailed in place. The reddish face veneer is damanu, a species from the Fiji Islands. Design: States Industries, Inc.

This Craftsman house has taken on an Oriental flavor. Walls bordered by teal-colored picture rail and trim pieces are simply mahogany plywood butt-joined and finished with tung oil; the frame trim is accented with black enamel. The ceiling features Chinese newspaper imprints peeled off still-tacky base paint; the process was the product of an inspirational accident. Interior design: Sherry Faure of Faure Design and Lila Levinson of Accent on Design.

MOLDINGS: DETAILS THAT MATTER

Built-up moldings add shape, depth, and grace to ¼-inch birch plywood panels. Architect: Remick Associates.

Profile upon profile is built up from basic molding patterns to create an elegant, formal cornice, smoothly seamed with caulking and white enamel. The "dragged" wallpaper softens the effect of the woodwork's clean, crisp lines. Interior design: Mona Branagh of Pacific Bay Interiors.

A frame within a frame lends prominence to the still life that hangs from a traditional picture rail capping frame-and-panel wainscoting. The highly figured paneling was given a new lease on life during a remodel of the entrance hall. Restoration: Steve Anderson of Wood Think It Was New.

A Look at Materials

Paneling a room, or even just one wall, is a dramatic way to improve the room's appearance; all you'll need for the job are some simple tools. The two main types of paneling are sheet and solid boards. Sheet paneling is easier to apply over large, unbroken surfaces because of its dimensions; solid boards, however, are simpler to fit around openings and obstructions.

Instructions for estimating and buying materials, preparing the surface, and putting up the paneling begin on the following page.

Sheet paneling

Sheet paneling is a catchall term for wall paneling that comes in large, machine-made panels—most commonly 4 by 8 feet. The two main types are *plywood* and *hardboard*. But when you look at a wall panel, you don't see plywood or hardboard. What you see is the panel's surface veneer, treated by the manufacturer in one of a wide variety of ways.

Plywood paneling. Plywood is manufactured from thin wood layers (veneers) peeled from the log with a very sharp cutter and then glued together. The grain of each veneer runs perpendicular to adjacent veneers, making plywood strong in all directions. Less expensive than most solid boards, plywood panels are also less subject to warping or shrinkage. They have a "sandwich" profile on the edges and real wood—usually lauan (Philippine mahogany)—on the back.

Generally speaking, any standard, unfinished plywood sheets may be used for wall paneling. But construction plywood isn't your only option. You can also find sheets expressly intended for paneling—you can buy just about any species of hardwood and most of the major softwoods laminated onto the surfaces of plywood panels. Prefinished and vinyl-faced decorative styles are also available, as are resin-coated panels designed for painting.

Plywood face textures range from highly polished to resawn; many types feature decorative grooves (often imitating solid-board patterns) and/or shiplap edges.

There are two standard thicknesses—¼ inch and ⁵⁄₁₆ inch. Avoid thinner panels—they're difficult to work with and not very durable.

Hardboard paneling. Hardboard is produced by reducing waste wood chips to fibers and then bonding the fibers back together under pressure with adhesives. A tough, pliable paneling, hardboard is sold in 4- by 8-foot sheets in thicknesses ranging from ³⁄₁₆ to ³⁄₈ inch; ¼ inch is usual.

Hardboard paneling is usually less expensive than plywood, but it's also less durable and more subject to warping or moisture damage.

The most common surface finishes are imitation wood; generally grooved to look like solid-board paneling, wood imitations are available in highly polished, resawn, or coarser brushed textures in a range of colors. You'll also see panels embossed with a pattern, such as basket weave, wicker, or louver.

Solid-board paneling

Texture, subtle variations in color and grain, imperfections, and natural fragrance make solid-board paneling particularly warm and inviting. It's especially suitable for areas where extensive handling and cutting are required, such as around doors, windows, and other large openings.

Solid-board paneling is, quite simply, any paneling made up of solid pieces of lumber positioned side by side. In some cases, standard, square-edged lumber is used—1 by 4s, 1 by 6s, and so forth. But generally, the boards have edges specially milled to overlap or interlock. The three basic millings—square edge, tongue-and-groove, and shiplap (or V-rustic)—are shown on page 122.

Hardwood boards are milled from such species as birch, cherry, mahogany, maple, oak, pecan, rosewood, teak, and walnut. Common softwoods include cedar, cypress, fir, hemlock, pine, redwood, and spruce.

Board thicknesses range from ¼ to ⅞ inch; widths range from 3 to 12 inches. Remember, though, that these are nominal—not actual—sizes (for details, see page 116). Standard boards range from 6 to 20 feet long.

Prepackaged ¼- or ⅜-inch-thick boards in random lengths are an increasingly popular choice; one package will cover about 32 square feet, the equivalent of a 4- by 8-foot plywood sheet. The boards can be glued or nailed directly over existing wallboard. For flexibility, they're reversible: one side is sanded and finished, the other is usually rough-sawn. These and other thin boards usually don't extend beyond the molding around doors and windows as the thicker 1-by boards do.

Moldings: The finishing touch

The absence of moldings, it's sometimes said, is a sign of good craftsmanship. Even in the most basic room, however, moldings have their place along the base of walls and around door and window frames.

Traditional wood moldings come in many standard patterns and sizes. You can buy them natural, prefinished (painted or stained), or wrapped with printed vinyl. Lengths range from 3 to 20 feet. For natural or stained molding, you'll probably want continuous, clear lengths. Painted and vinyl-wrapped moldings are often shorter lengths finger-jointed at their ends to make longer pieces; they can be much less expensive than clear pieces. Ponderosa pine is the most popular material; oak is a common hardwood choice.

Strips or boards—for example, clear redwood, fir, or pine 1 by 2s, 1 by 4s, or 1 by 6s—make handsome, bold trim over paneling.

You can also find plastic, vinyl, or aluminum moldings that look like wood. Integral molding systems include corner pieces that eliminate the need for tricky corner cuts and joints.

First Things First

Before you climb into your working clothes, you'll need to measure the area to be paneled, estimate the amount of paneling and molding you'll need, buy the material, condition it, and gather the necessary tools and equipment.

If you're a newcomer to the lumberyard, the information below will provide you with a crash course.

Estimating & buying materials

When thinking about the kind of paneling you want, keep in mind some facts about cost. Prices for solid boards vary with availability; for example, redwood is considerably less expensive in some Western areas than it is on the East Coast. Generally, solid-board paneling is more expensive than sheet paneling. To keep costs down, choose a species or pattern that's stocked locally. Extras such as transportation and special milling can run quite high.

Estimating for board paneling or for complex sheet installations. To begin, measure the wall or walls you plan to panel, using a steel tape measure. Then make a scale drawing of the area on graph paper and transfer the figures to the drawing. Add any windows, doors, or other large openings to the drawing and note their dimensions.

Figure the total wall area by multiplying the wall's height by its width. From this amount, subtract the area of all openings.

Then, decide on the pattern of application (for solid-board paneling, see pages 122–123) and the size and milling of the boards you want. Using your square-footage figures and sketches, your dealer can compute the amount of materials you'll need. It's customary to add 5 to 10 percent to your order for waste and mistakes.

Measuring for sheet paneling. If the wall you're paneling is a standard 8-foot height, figuring the number of panels you'll need is easy. Just measure the width of the wall in feet and divide by the width of your paneling. Round fractions up to the next whole number.

If your wall is higher than 8 feet, order extra-long panels or allow for extra panels to fill out the height. Chances are any seams will be inconspicuous; if not, you can cover them with molding.

Unless a very large part of the wall is windows and doors, don't bother

Lumberyard Lingo

If you're not well versed in the language of the lumberyard, shopping for lumber can be overwhelming at first. Here's some information to help you out.

Lumber sizes. Most beginners assume that a 1 by 6 is 1 inch thick by 6 inches wide. It's not. Such numbers give the nominal size of the lumber; when the piece is dried and surfaced (planed), it's reduced to a smaller size.

The chart below gives nominal and actual sizes of standard lumber.

Nominal Size	Surfaced (Actual) Size
1 by 2	¾" by 1½"
1 by 3	¾" by 2½"
1 by 4	¾" by 3½"
1 by 6	¾" by 5½"
1 by 8	¾" by 7¼"
1 by 10	¾" by 9¼"
1 by 12	¾" by 11¼"

Hardwood or softwood? Lumber is divided into hardwoods and softwoods, terms that refer to the origin of the wood. Hardwood paneling is milled from broad-leafed, deciduous trees, such as mahogany, oak, and walnut. Softwoods come from evergreens (conifers) like fir, pine, and redwood.

Although hardwoods are usually more durable than softwoods, some softwoods—like Douglas fir and Southern pine—are actually harder than such so-called hardwoods as poplar, aspen, or lauan (Philippine mahogany). As a rule, softwoods are much less expensive, easier to tool, and more readily available than hardwoods.

Lumber grades. For practical purposes, most board paneling can be termed clear or knotty. Clear softwood paneling boards normally correspond to any formal Select or Finish board grade, knotty panels to Common 2 and 3 grades. Some species, such as redwood and Southern pine, have their own designations. Boards may be surfaced either smooth or resawn (rough).

Vertical or flat grain? Depending on the cut of the millsaw, lumber will have either parallel grain lines running the length of the piece (vertical grain) or a marbled appearance (flat grain). When you can, choose vertical-grain paneling; it's less likely to warp or shrink, and it looks better, too. Some vertical grain lumber commands a premium price.

Moisture content. When wood is sawn, it's still "green"—that is, unseasoned. Before it's ready for use, most lumber is dried, either by air-drying or kiln-drying. To avoid shrinkage and cupping, always look for kiln-dried ("KD") boards.

to deduct for them. It's much easier to cut window and door areas from whole sheets than to piece around openings.

Ordering moldings. Remember that with moldings, thickness is specified first, width second, and length last. For example, a piece of molding may be ⅜ inch thick by 2¼ inches wide by 8 feet long. Both thickness and width are measured at their widest point.

Conditioning paneling

Plan to store paneling in the room to be paneled for at least 2 days, preferably up to 10 days, so it can adapt to room temperature and humidity. Stack paneling on the floor, separating each piece with 2 by 4s or with furring strips.

The basic toolbox

To install paneling, you may only need a few basic carpentry tools: steel tape measure, combination square, handsaw, block plane, hammer, nailset, drill, and pencil. If you're putting up sheets with adhesive, add a caulking gun. A belt sander corrects minor fit problems.

A few specialized tools can make the work go faster. A carpenter's level helps you inspect the surface and keep the paneling on course; a chalk line makes long, straight guidelines. A stud finder helps locate studs, and a prybar and utility knife pry off moldings.

If your job requires a lot of cutting, it's helpful to have a power saw—a portable circular saw for sheets, a power miter saw (narrow cuts) or radial-arm saw (wider cuts) for crosscutting solid boards. A saber saw or keyhole saw cuts odd shapes and finishes off corners and cutouts. To cut moldings you'll need a stiff, sharp backsaw and miter box or a power miter saw. A coping saw's thin, wiry blade cuts curves and is handy for complex molding profiles.

Tools for paneling include (1) power miter saw, (2) backsaw and miter box, (3) caulking gun, (4) saber saw, (5) portable circular saw, (6) electric drill, (7) combination square, (8) belt sander, (9) claw hammer, (10) tape measure, (11) chalk line, (12) keyhole saw, (13) carpenter's level, (14) prybar, (15) block plane, (16) utility knife, (17) stud finder, (18) nailsets, (19) coping saw.

Preparing the Surface

Like painting, wallpapering, and most other interior finishing approaches, a successful paneling job requires careful preparation of the surface to be covered. Be sure to complete all necessary preparations before you begin installing any paneling.

Removing moldings & baseboards

The first step is to remove all moldings, baseboards, and base shoes (the oval-shaped strips sometimes nailed to baseboards). If you plan to reuse the molding material, be careful to avoid marring or splitting as you remove it. If your trim is painted, score the paint seams with a utility knife before using the prybar.

Most moldings are attached with finishing nails. To remove a section of molding, hammer a thin, broad-bladed prybar behind it, as shown in the drawing at right, and gently pry outward until the molding begins to give. Then move the bar over a few inches and repeat the process until the entire piece comes loose. Hammer in any nails remaining in the wall or pull them out with pliers.

Locating & marking wall studs

Most walls are not solid—they're made of gypsum wallboard, plaster and lath, or wood paneling laid over a framework of studs and plates. (For an overview of wall anatomy, see the drawing below.) In most cases, you'll have to locate the studs hidden within the wall before you can attach the paneling.

Studs, vertical 2 by 4s or 2 by 6s, are normally spaced either 16 or 24 inches apart, center to center. Often,

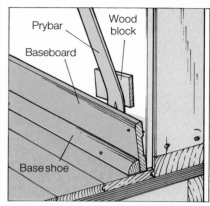

Protecting wall with a wood block, gently pry molding from wall, using a prybar.

you can simply start from one of the four major house corners, measure in 14½ inches, and find the first stud there. Check the wall for evidence of wallboard compound or nail heads. If no nails show, try using a stud finder.

If all else fails, probe into the wall about 2 inches above the floor (be sure you're above the soleplate), using a long nail or drill.

Once you've found one stud, locating the rest should be easy. Measure 16 or 24 inches from that point to find the next stud. To mark the stud centers, draw a light line in pencil or chalk on the floor and ceiling so the marks will be visible once the panel is in place.

Preparing the wall

For a successful job, the wall being paneled must be fairly flat and plumb. To determine flatness, hold a long, straight 2 by 4 against the wall, moving it over the entire surface. To see if the wall is plumb, use a carpenter's level.

If the wall is flat and plumb and you're using an adhesive to install the paneling, simply clean the wall thoroughly with an ordinary household cleaner or a specialized wall-cleaning product. If the wall is plumb but a little bumpy or damaged, you can nail paneling directly to the wall, provided there are subsurface studs, sills, and headers to which you can nail it.

If the wall is very bumpy or significantly out of plumb, you'll need to apply furring strips, as described on the facing page.

■ WALL FRAMING COMPONENTS

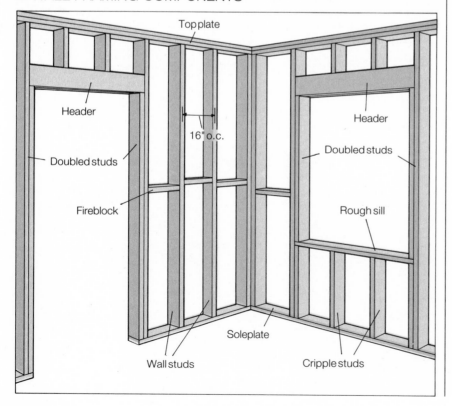

Top plate

Header

16" o.c.

Doubled studs

Fireblock

Header

Doubled studs

Rough sill

Soleplate

Wall studs

Cripple studs

■ THREE FURRING ARRANGEMENTS

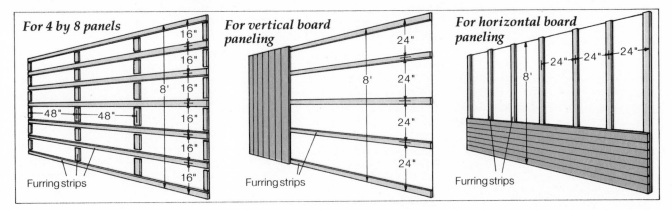

For 4 by 8 panels
16"
16"
8' 16"
48" 48"
16"
16"
16"
Furring strips

For vertical board paneling
24"
24"
8' 24"
24"
24"
Furring strips

For horizontal board paneling
24" 24" 24"
8'
Furring strips

A wall made of masonry should be waterproofed before you apply the paneling. Patch the surface with cement grout and then apply a waterproofing sealer. A vapor barrier paper or polyester film between the masonry and furring strips will further protect the paneling from moisture.

Furring & shimming

You'll need to install a framework of furring strips if your wall is very bumpy or severely damaged, if it's significantly out of plumb, or if you need suitably spaced subsurface wall members for nailing. The strips, usually 1 by 2s or 1 by 3s, provide a good nailing or gluing surface for paneling.

The arrangement of the furring strips depends on the type of paneling

being applied and, in the case of board paneling, its direction. Three arrangements are shown above.

To apply the strips, follow the steps shown below. For wood-frame walls, nails should penetrate at least 1 inch into the studs. For masonry walls, use concrete nails or expansion bolts. To allow for future house shifting or settling, always leave a ¼-inch space at the top and bottom of the wall when you're applying furring strips.

Of course, furring strips should be plumb and flat; when the furring is in place, check for flatness using a long, straight 2 by 4. Mark the areas that sag inward.

You can make small adjustments with shingle shims, as shown. Simply tap them into place until the furring is flat and/or plumb; then nail through

the furring to keep the shims from falling out. If the existing wall is severely out of plumb, you may need to block out furring strips at one end.

When you add furring strips, you'll also need to adjust door and window frames and the boxes for receptacles and switches to accommodate the increased wall thickness.

To adjust door and window frames, simply add extension jambs or other material of sufficient thickness to the existing trim. Take care to match surfaces so that painting will cover the joint between the old and new material.

Metal electrical boxes require some effort to pry loose; instead, consider adding a metal extension sleeve (available at an electrical supply store) to the front of the box. Turn off the power to the room before removing any boxes.

■ INSTALLING FURRING STRIPS

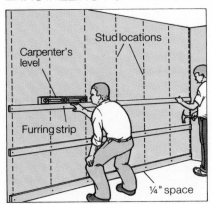

Stud locations
Carpenter's level
Furring strip
¼" space

Find and mark stud locations. Tack one end of a furring strip to a stud ¼ inch from bottom of wall. Check for level at other end; nail strip to stud. Continue applying strips.

Straight 2 by 4
Nail strip to each stud

To check for flatness, hold a long, straight 2 by 4 against furring strip. If strip is flat, finish nailing strip to studs between corners, using one nail for each stud.

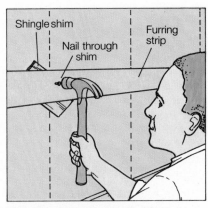

Shingle shim
Nail through shim
Furring strip

Remove slight irregularities by driving tapered shims behind furring. Tap shims into place until strips are flat and/or plumb; then nail shims to wall through furring.

Sheet Paneling

Sheet paneling—typically decorative plywood or hardboard—can be laid over new stud walls, applied directly to existing walls in good condition, or attached to furring strips over old, bumpy walls. If you're paneling over bare studs, ask your dealer 'whether you'll need to back the sheets with gypsum wallboard or another material for rigidity and fire protection.

Cutting the sheets

Before you begin cutting, check to see if the room's ceiling height varies. Then allow for a ¼-inch clearance between the paneling and the floor so the panels won't buckle as the house settles.

To make safe, efficient saw cuts, you must support your sheet material securely. In a well-equipped shop you'll have no problem, but if you're using a handsaw or portable power saw, you'll need a pair of sturdy sawhorses or their equivalent. Bridge the two sawhorses with scrap 2 by 4s, as shown in the illustration at right.

If you're cutting with a portable circular saw, set the blade depth so that you cut through the material but just nick the scrap. With a handsaw, cut only up to the scrap support. Slide the sheet forward slightly for a little more unobstructed cutting; then reposition the sheet and continue cutting on the other side of the support.

Sometimes, ripping requires only two sawhorses and no scrap supports. However, thin sheets will need support near the cutting line to prevent sagging.

If it's hard to keep the saw on a straight line, clamp a straightedge along the cutting line (for a handsaw) or the width of the baseplate away (for a portable power saw), and let the saw ride against it.

For a good appearance, cut the first and last panels on a wall the same width, unless you're using panels with random-width grooves. Prop up the panels along the wall to see how they'll look. Whenever possible, center between-panel joints over door and window openings. At inside corners, plan to butt panels together. Outside corners, unless perfectly mitered, will require two pieces of trim or a premilled corner molding (see page 122).

Attaching the paneling

Although it's possible to apply sheet paneling with nails alone, using an adhesive and then securing the ends of the panel with finishing nails is the most common approach. Adhesive is fast and clean, and it reduces the risk of denting or otherwise damaging the panels. Solvent or water-base paneling adhesive is typically packaged in 11-ounce cartridges and is applied with a caulking gun.

Here's the typical procedure. First, cut a panel ¼ inch shorter than the distance from floor to ceiling. On a finished wall, apply adhesive directly to the wall, spacing it in squiggly lines a uniform 12 or 16 inches apart. On furring strips or exposed wall framing, apply squiggly stripes of adhesive to the framing.

Drive four finishing nails through the top edge of the panel—4-penny nails for ¼-inch panels, 6-penny for panels up to ⅝ inch thick, and 8-penny for thicker materials. Position the panel on the wall, leaving a ¼-inch space at the bottom; drive the nails partway

■ SUPPORT FOR SAFE CUTTING

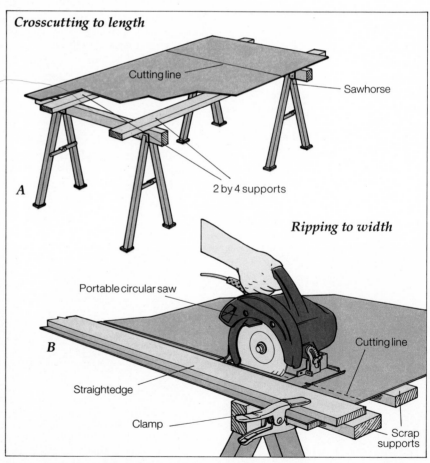

Crosscutting to length

Cutting line

Sawhorse

2 by 4 supports

A

Ripping to width

Portable circular saw

Cutting line

Straightedge

B

Clamp

Scrap supports

To support sheet paneling evenly, bridge two sawhorses with scrap lumber. To crosscut with a circular saw, set blade depth to just nick 2 by 4s and cut panel (A); when ripping, use a straightedge to help guide cut (B).

into the wall to act as hinge pins. Pull the panel's bottom edge about 6 inches out from the wall and push a block behind it to hold it there.

Wait for the adhesive to become tacky (check the manufacturer's directions). Then remove the block and press the panel firmly into place. To force the adhesive into tight contact, carefully tap the panel with a rubber mallet or use a hammer against a padded block.

Drive the nails all the way in; then nail the panels at the bottom. (You'll eventually cover the nail heads and the ¼-inch gap with molding.) Thin paneling materials require additional adhesive or nails within ½ inch of the panel edges to prevent curling.

Scribing a panel. Any piece of paneling that you fit into a corner probably won't exactly match the contours of the adjoining wall or obstruction. To duplicate the irregularities of the adjoining surface on the paneling's edge, prop the panel into place about an inch from the uneven surface.

Then run a small wood block and pencil, as shown in the drawing below, at right, along the irregular surface so the pencil duplicates the unevenness onto the paneling.

Cut the paneling along the scribed line with a coping saw, saber saw, belt sander, or block plane.

Cutting an opening. Fitting a panel around a door or window opening or an electrical box requires careful measuring, marking, and cutting.

Keep track of all the measurements by sketching them on a piece of paper.

When taking vertical measurements, remember that you'll install the paneling ¼ inch above the floor.

Marking the side of the panel that will face you as you cut (face up for a handsaw, face down for a portable power saw), transfer these measurements to the panel. (If you're marking the back of the panel, remember that measurements will be a mirror image of the opening.)

Cut large openings following the cutting directions on the facing page; you may need to finish a corner with a handsaw or saber saw. To make cutouts in panels for small openings, drill holes in the panel in opposite corners of the opening you've marked, as shown below. Then cut the opening, cutting from the front with a keyhole saw, from the back with a saber saw.

■ PUTTING UP THE PANELING

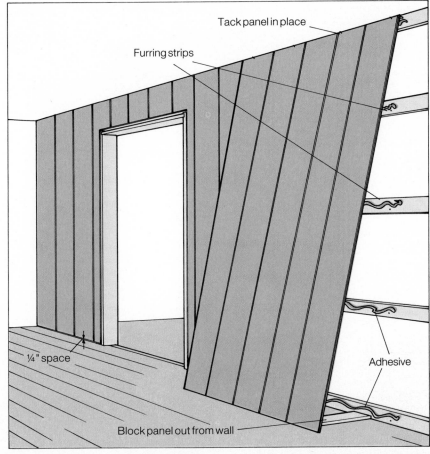

To install a panel, apply adhesive to furring strips or to wall. Tack sheet in place along top edge; then prop it out from wall as shown. When adhesive becomes tacky, press panel into place and finish nailing along bottom.

■ FITTING TECHNIQUES

To fit a panel to an irregular surface, pull it slightly away from corner; scribe along edge with a wood block and pencil. Cut along the scribed line with a saw, belt sander, or block plane.

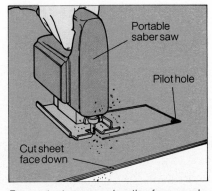

For a cutout, measure location from panel edge and end. Drill pilot holes in opposite corners; cut with a saber or keyhole saw.

Paneling **121**

Solid-Board Paneling

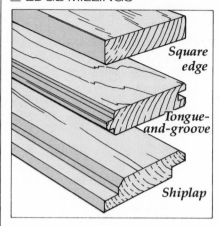

Square edge

Tongue-and-groove

Shiplap

Like sheet paneling, solid boards can be attached to new stud walls, to existing walls that are in good shape, or to a gridwork of furring strips applied over old, bumpy walls.

Although solid boards are usually installed vertically or horizontally, don't limit your options. For added visual punch, consider a diagonal pattern or one designed for exterior siding.

Basic techniques

Regardless of the pattern you choose for your paneling, solid boards are cut and applied in much the same way.

Cutting boards. Most solid-board applications simply require cutting boards to length. If you're operating a handsaw or portable circular saw, first use a combination square to mark 90° or 45° end cuts. Otherwise, a miter saw or radial-arm saw will do it all very accurately with one adjustment.

If you need to rip (cut boards to width) the first and last boards, a sharp rip saw, a portable circular saw with an edge guide, and a table saw are all good tools. You cut solid boards to fit into corners and around openings the same way as you do sheet paneling (see page 121).

To prevent splintering, place finished boards face up if you're cutting them with a handsaw, power miter saw, or radial-arm saw, face down if you're using a portable circular or saber saw.

Fastening boards. You can either nail solid boards to your wall surface or attach them with adhesive. Nailing is the preferred method. For standard 1-by boards, plan to use 6-penny finishing nails and recess the heads below the surface with a nailset. Cover the nail heads, using a putty stick in a matching color. One shop tip: To nail up paneling quickly without damaging it, use a squeeze-type nail gun (a common rental item). One squeeze and this tool will countersink a nail.

Where you nail depends on the panel's milling. Typical edge millings and nailing options are shown at right.

If you use an adhesive, apply it as described for sheet paneling (see pages 120–121), following the manufacturer's directions. Also nail the top and bottom of each board after gluing.

Vertical paneling

Before paneling vertically with solid boards, you must attach horizontal furring strips to the wall every 24 inches on center (see page 119); or install nailing blocks at those spacings between studs.

Measure the width of the boards you're using and then the width of the wall. From these figures, calculate the width of the final board. To avoid a sliver-size board, split the difference so the first and last boards are the same width. Plan to cut boards ¼ inch shorter than the height from floor to ceiling to allow for any house shifting or settling in the future.

When you place the first board into the corner, check the edge with a carpenter's level. If the board isn't plumb or doesn't fit the corner exactly, scribe and trim the edge facing the corner as for sheet paneling (see page 121).

Attach the first board, leaving a ¼-inch space above the floor; then slide the second board against its edge and, if it's tongue-and-groove milling, use a scrap block of the same material to help drive the tongue home. Check the board for plumb before you nail. Repeat this procedure with all subsequent boards. To fit the last board easily into place, cut its edge at a slight angle (about 5°) toward the back edge of the board, as shown in the illustration at the top of the facing page.

At inside corners, simply butt adjacent boards together, scribing if necessary. At outside corners, there are three options, shown at right: you can miter the joints for a neat fit (cut the miters at an angle slightly greater than

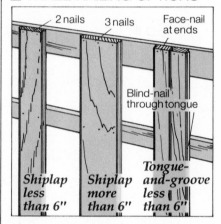

2 nails   3 nails   Face-nail at ends

Blind-nail through tongue

Shiplap less than 6"   *Shiplap more than 6"*   *Tongue-and-groove less than 6"*

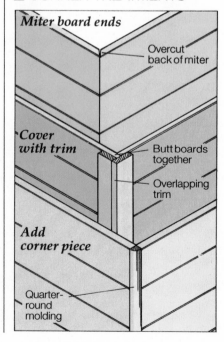

Miter board ends

Overcut back of miter

Cover with trim

Butt boards together

Overlapping trim

Add corner piece

Quarter-round molding

■ BOARD INSTALLATION: VERTICAL PATTERN

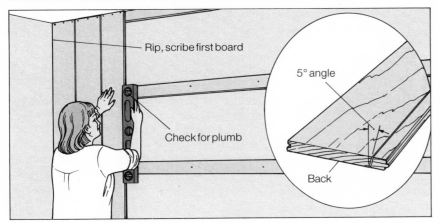

Rip, scribe first board

5° angle

Check for plumb

Back

Rip first board as required, prop it in place, and check for plumb; scribe and trim edge, if necessary. Nail in place. Add subsequent boards, checking each for plumb as you go. To make last board fit, cut edge slightly toward board's back side (see inset).

■ BOARD INSTALLATION: HORIZONTAL PATTERN

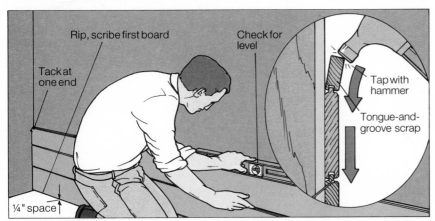

Rip, scribe first board

Check for level

Tack at one end

Tap with hammer

Tongue-and-groove scrap

¼" space

Position first board ¼ inch above floor, tack at one end, and check for level. Then secure far end. Add additional boards on top, checking for level as you go. To seat a stubborn tongue in its groove, use a scrap block of same material (see inset).

■ BOARD INSTALLATION: DIAGONAL PATTERN

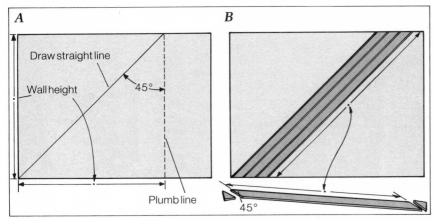

A

Draw straight line

45°

Wall height

Plumb line

B

45°

From corner, measure out wall height, draw a plumb line, and draw a diagonal line from corner to top of plumb line (A). Cut first piece to length of diagonal line, cutting ends at a 45° angle. Measure leading edge (B) to cut remaining boards.

45° so they'll fit snugly), conceal the joint with trim, or run the boards up to corner pieces.

Horizontal paneling

Generally, you won't need to apply furring if you're attaching boards horizontally, unless the wall is badly damaged or out of plumb. You can nail the boards to the studs directly or through existing wall coverings. To avoid ending with a very narrow board at the ceiling, calculate its size and split the difference so the lowest and highest boards are the same width.

Start at the bottom of the wall and work toward the ceiling. Temporarily nail the first board at one end, ¼ inch above the floor. Then level the board and complete the nailing. If needed, scribe and trim the board as for sheet paneling (see page 121). Minor inconsistencies can be covered with molding.

Working toward the ceiling, attach each board in the same way (see at left). Rip the last board to width, leaving a slight space below the ceiling. If you have trouble fitting the last board, bevel its back edge slightly and pivot it into place.

Diagonal paneling

When boards are installed correctly, this pattern appears to run from one wall onto the next. Boards are usually installed at a 45° angle unless the room's shape or style suggests an alternative. Furring isn't needed unless the wall is badly damaged or out of plumb.

In the corner where you want to begin, measure the height of the wall from floor to ceiling. Measure the same distance across the bottom of the wall and mark the wall at that point. Using a level, draw a plumb line directly above the mark and make another mark at the top of the wall (see at left). With a straight board, draw a line from the bottom corner to the mark at the top; this line should form a 45° angle.

Measure the length of the line and transfer that measurement to a length of board paneling. Cut the board and nail or glue it into place. Measure, mark, cut, and attach each additional board in the same way.

Moldings & Trim

Contoured moldings or standard lumber trim fastened along the bottom edge of wallboard or wood paneling covers the gaps between the wall covering and the floor. Used at the ceiling line and in corners, moldings add elegance. At the edges of door and window openings, they finish off the framing.

Shown below are some standard molding patterns and their common applications. It's likely that you'll find many more choices at a well-stocked dealer; some specialists will also mill custom profiles or match existing patterns. Specialty moldings are also available by mail order.

If you have access to a shaper, or even a portable router and router table, you can make your own contours from standard lumber. For ideas on how to combine simple moldings in order to create classic or custom effects, turn to page 127.

Basic techniques

A first-rate molding installation requires careful measuring, cutting, and fastening. This is especially true if you plan to apply stain or a clear finish to the wood. (Mistakes can be corrected with caulk on painted moldings.) Here

are some tricks of the trade that will result in a neat, clean job.

Measuring and cutting molding. When you're measuring for miters—to frame a window, for example—measure the inside dimensions and cut your material accordingly (that is, adding on the mitered part). Remember that you must reverse the cuts on the ends of each piece of molding. One tip: The distance the miter extends is roughly equal to 1½ times the width of the molding; be prepared to do some fine-tuning when fitting.

Traditionally, a miter box and backsaw are the tools for neatly cutting trim. But if you're making lots of cuts or working with unusual angles, it may be worthwhile to borrow or rent a power miter saw. The precision miter saw allows you to cut the trim a bit

■ MOLDING PROFILES

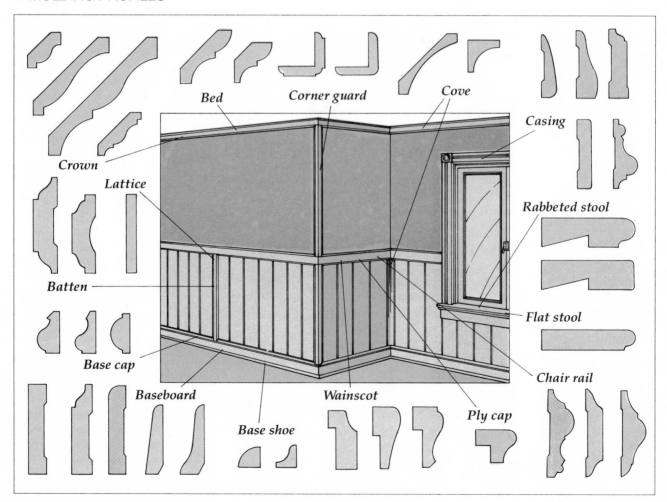

Crown · Bed · Corner guard · Cove · Casing · Lattice · Rabbeted stool · Batten · Flat stool · Base cap · Chair rail · Baseboard · Wainscot · Ply cap · Base shoe

■ COPING A JOINT

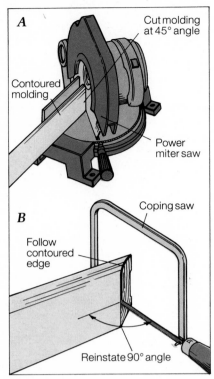

A — Cut molding at 45° angle
Contoured molding
Power miter saw

B — Coping saw
Follow contoured edge
Reinstate 90° angle

For a neat coped joint, first miter end at a 45° angle, using a power miter saw (A) or a backsaw and miter box. Then follow shape of exposed edge with a coping saw while reinstating original 90° angle (B).

■ BASEBOARD & CEILING JOINTS

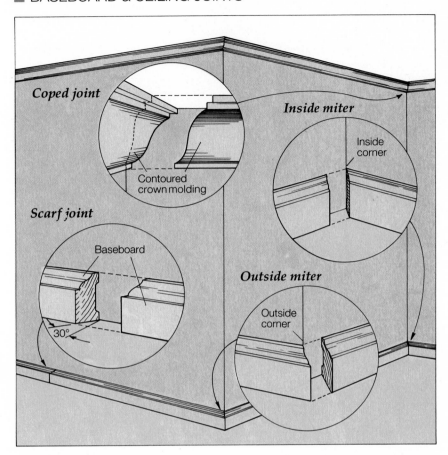

Coped joint — Contoured crown molding
Inside miter — Inside corner
Scarf joint — Baseboard — 30°
Outside miter — Outside corner

---

long and then nibble fine bits of wood until the joint is perfect.

Contoured moldings may require a coped joint at inside corners for a smooth fit. To form a coped joint, cut the first piece of molding square and butt it into the corner. Then cut the end of the second piece back at a 45° angle, as shown above.

Next, using a coping saw, follow the exposed curvature of the molding's front edge while reinstating the 90° angle. With a little practice, you can make the contoured end smoothly match the first piece.

Fastening moldings. Unless your molding calls for special adhesive or color-matched fasteners, nail it in place with finishing nails and recess the heads with a nailset.

If you'll be painting the trim, fill the holes with wood putty; if you're staining or varnishing, apply a color-matched filler *after* finishing.

When nailing hardwoods, predrill the molding to prevent it from splitting. Use a drill bit slightly smaller in diameter than the finishing nail, and drill through the molding and just into the framing member behind.

Baseboards & ceiling moldings

Once any new finish floor is installed, you can attach baseboards and, if desired, base shoes. Leave a slight gap between the flooring and the bottom of the molding when you're installing these pieces; thin cardboard works well as a spacer. Be sure to nail the moldings to the wall studs and soleplate, *not* to the floor.

Two helpful hints: Make a dry run to determine fit, and use the longest molding pieces you can to help bridge uneven areas.

Where two lengths of molding join along a wall, miter the ends to create a

scarf joint, as shown in the drawing above. Nail through the joint to secure the pieces.

For contoured moldings, cut a coped joint at inside corners. At outside corners, simply cut matching miters in each piece, as shown. (Cut away the underside of the material when you're using thick stock so that the outer, or visible, edge of the molding will fit tightly.)

Out-of-square corners can cause havoc with tight-fitting joints; you may have to fine-tune the angle, undercut the back edges, or slip small cardboard or wood shims behind the joint. If you're painting, you can always caulk or putty the joint closed.

Install ceiling moldings the same way as baseboards. Ceiling lines are almost never perfectly even, so plan to space the molding slightly below the seam; cover any gaps with caulk and paint. Again, fasten these moldings to the wall framing, not to the ceiling.

Paneling **125**

■ DOOR & WINDOW CASINGS

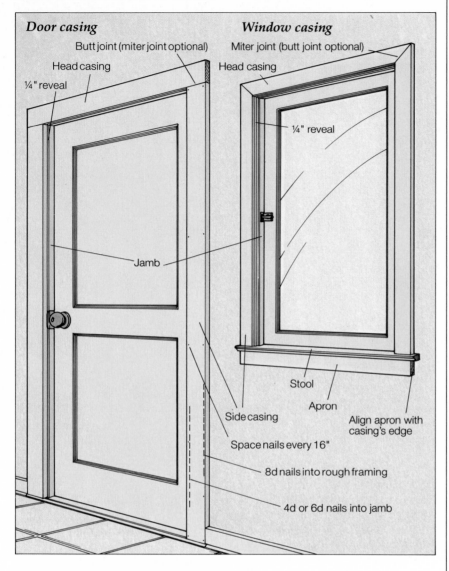

Door casing

Butt joint (miter joint optional)

Head casing

¼" reveal

Jamb

Side casing

Space nails every 16"

8d nails into rough framing

4d or 6d nails into jamb

Window casing

Miter joint (butt joint optional)

Head casing

¼" reveal

Stool

Apron

Align apron with casing's edge

■ MARKING A WINDOW STOOL

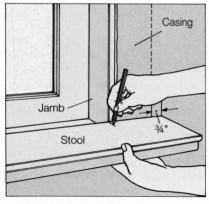

Casing

Jamb

Stool

¾"

Aligning end of stool with mark on wall, hold stool up to a side jamb and mark inside edge of jamb on stool's back edge.

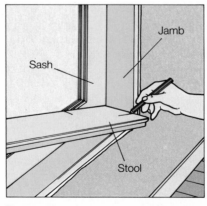

Jamb

Sash

Stool

Then position stool against jamb flush with sash and mark jamb's front edge on stool. Extend marks until they intersect.

Ornate ceiling patterns and crown moldings are often a composite of two or more molding profiles piled on top of one another. Several ideas are illustrated on the facing page.

Door casings

Door trim may be made of either contoured molding or standard lumber. If you choose lumber, plan to butt joints together at the top; for molding, you'll have to miter the joints.

Before installing the casing, pencil a reveal, or setback line, ¼ inch in from the inside edge of each jamb, as shown at left. Aligning the head casing with the pencil line, mark it where it intersects the side reveal lines. Miter the ends from these points or, if you prefer, add the width of the side casings and cut the ends square.

Use 4- or 6-penny finishing nails to attach the casing to the jamb, and 8-penny nails along the rough framing. Space nails every 16 inches.

Now measure for the side casing. If the door jambs are level and plumb, all should join snugly. If not, you'll have to adjust the angles of the side cuts to fit the top casing exactly. Then nail the side casings into position. If the finish floor is not yet in place, be sure to leave room for it at the bottom of the casings.

Window casings

Most window units require interior trim around the opening. Standard treatment consists of head and side casings, a stool atop the finish sill, and a bottom casing, or apron, below the stool.

Begin by penciling a ⅛- or ¼-inch reveal just inside the side and head jambs; then measure the width of your casing. Adding ¾ inch to the casing's width, measure this distance out from each side jamb's reveal and make a mark on the wall.

Now measure the distance between these marks: this is the length you'll cut the stool. Use either a flat piece of lumber or a preformed rabbeted or flat stool to match the slope of the finish sill.

Position the stool so its ends align with the marks on the wall, as shown in the drawing at left; then mark the inside edge of each side jamb on the stool's back edge.

Place one end of the stool against a jamb (keep the back edge flush with the window's sash) and mark the jamb's front edge on the stool. Repeat this process for the other end.

Using a combination square, extend each set of marks until they intersect; then notch the stool along the lines. Set the stool in place and fasten it to the finish sill with 6-penny finishing nails.

Next, square off one end of a piece of casing. Set that end on the stool, aligning the inside edge with the reveal. Mark the inside edge of the casing where the head jamb's reveal crosses it. If you're using contoured molding, cut the end at a 45° miter. For flat lumber, cut the end square.

Nail the casing to the jamb with 4-penny finishing nails, and to the rough framing with 8-penny nails. Repeat this process for the other side casing.

For the casing at the top, cut one end of another piece of molding to fit the side casing. Make a trial fit; then cut as necessary so the casing follows the reveal line. At the other end, make another trial fit; if all is well, cut the casing to length and nail it in place.

For the apron, cut a piece of molding to the length between the outsides of the side casings. Center the apron under the stool and nail it to the rough framing with 6-penny finishing nails.

Winning Combinations

If you've ever gazed upon ornate period ceilings, dining room wainscoting, or details around mantels or fireplace surrounds, you may have come away with a mixture of inspiration and intimidation. Some of this millwork is truly custom-made, but upon closer inspection, you'll be surprised at how often these woodworking wonders can be reduced to simple, readily available components—wholes that add up to more than their separate parts.

Below, we've pictured several popular treatments. But keep your eyes open; as you move about and make acquaintance with common molding profiles, no doubt you'll discover quite a few more winning combinations.

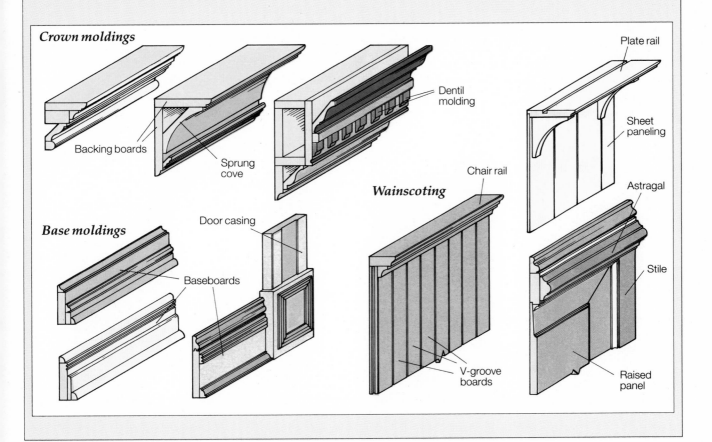

Crown moldings

Backing boards

Sprung cove

Dentil molding

Plate rail

Sheet paneling

Chair rail

Wainscoting

Astragal

Base moldings

Door casing

Baseboards

V-groove boards

Stile

Raised panel

Index

Bold numbers refer to photographs that show decorative wall coverings in use.